Educating Business Professionals

Educating Business Professionals

The Call Beyond Competence and Expertise

Lana S. Nino, PhD
Susan D. Gotsch, PhD

BEP BUSINESS EXPERT PRESS

Educating Business Professionals: The Call Beyond Competence and Expertise
Copyright © Business Expert Press, LLC, 2017.

First published in 2017 by
Business Expert Press, LLC
222 East 46th Street, New York, NY 10017
www.businessexpertpress.com

ISBN-13: 978-1-63157-319-4 (print)
ISBN-13: 978-1-63157-320-0 (e-book)

Business Expert Press Giving Voice to Values on Business Ethics and Corporate Social Responsibility Collection

Collection ISSN: 2333-8806 (print)
Collection ISSN: 2333-8814 (electronic)

Cover and interior design by S4Carlisle Publishing Services Private Ltd., Chennai, India

First edition: 2017

10 9 8 7 6 5 4 3 2 1

Printed in the United States of America

Dedication

To all our wonderful donors, colleagues, and students who made this possible. Because of your support, dedication, and creativity, the road to a better business world should be two steps nearer.

Abstract

Given the influential role that business professionals now play in society, high-quality education is essential. A recognition that business programs can and should nurture leaders committed not only to personal and corporate success but also to social progress rests at the core of a revised and renewed education model.

Steeped in the liberal arts, this book presents a practical plan to achieve that goal. It makes a cogent argument for incorporating a theoretical model of professionalism into undergraduate and graduate business programs, and offers guidance to business deans and faculty interested in preparing students for the evolving role of business leadership in the 21st century. Using an adapted "wheel of professionalism" model, it describes curricular content and educational approaches designed to guide students toward higher levels of professionalism, social consciousness, and ethical decision-making.

Contents

List of Figures

Foreword

For several decades, business schools have been the center of discussions that urge needed improvements in how and what is taught. The driving force for this change is the need for more ethical, socially responsible business managers running our companies and benefiting society. Almost everyone agrees on the needed change. But how does higher education, while adjusting to rapid expansion and economic pressure, achieve higher aspirations and more professional qualities for business students? This is where the old framework of "professionalism" may help solve a new and evolving problem. The nature of professions and professional education are particularly interesting subjects to address what is needed to improve business education. While the field of business has claimed the status of a "profession," it has not closely examined the ideals and responsibilities that are intertwined with that status.

The current challenges are many, often because of the expansion of knowledge that business students need to master for their careers. Our book uses the concepts embedded in the definition of "profession" to begin to make the needed changes toward business professional education. We provide practical approaches that employ established and accepted practices used in other professions, such as medicine and nursing, but adapt them to the business discipline. Although the goal of professionalism does not end with undergraduate studies, this book was written with undergraduates in mind. Both authors teach at the undergraduate level, and therefore the techniques and approaches used targeted this group of students. However, there is a similar opportunity to utilize the platform of professionalism at the graduate level.

The book used Miller's (1985) theoretical framework, namely the "Wheel of Professionalism" to build a model of recommended changes. Although the authors, for the most part, have used these approaches at their college, the book only recommends the suggested approaches—to the degree they can be adapted to various environments and programs.

We hope that deans, administrators, and faculty involved in business programs at colleges and universities benefit from our work and adapt it to their programs.

The implementation of the book can be done in part or as a whole. For improvements in ethics education, Chapters 4 and 5 provide several suggestions. For more significant improvements toward professionalism, starting at Chapter 3 is important, in addition to reviewing the resources that we used to develop our methodology, which are listed in the references. For ideas on infusing theory, interdisciplinary learning, and leadership, Chapters 6 and 7 provide a wealth of examples. Finally, for adding a social agency component to a business program, Chapter 8 is good resource.

In the last chapter, the authors explain how they have been able to implement many changes within the business program and outline the steps to start on this path. We recognize that our work at Whittier College was to embed liberal arts approaches into our business curriculum. In that process, issues of ethical behavior and decision-making, analysis from multiple points of view, and engagement with the community were important. As Lana, and later Susan, began to see the connections to the "professional" model, we confirmed that what we were doing and the many ideas that were generated could be useful in the wider discussions about changing the education of undergraduate business majors. The extensive literature on professions suggested some of the same approaches that are at the core of the liberal arts. That "aha" moment was the start of our collaboration on this book.

Below is a brief description of the structure of the book. The first part covers the historical background of how the business discipline evolved, as well as theoretical models to study professionals. The goal of the first part is to understand how business education can incorporate a model of professionalism, as well as how business students compare to other students relative to the elements of the professional model namely, expertise, autonomy of judgment, self-concept, and social agency.

In the second part, the model uses the "wheel of professionalism" to present the curricular elements that are essential to achieve higher levels of professionalism. These elements include a foundation of ethics with repeating themes, multi-framing and leadership studies, theory development, research and continuous knowledge building, and community service orientation. The chapter explains each of the elements, as well as its importance for the professional development of business students.

In the third part, we recommend a separate course for building a foundation in ethics with a focus on the individual, the student, rather than the corporation and its stakeholders. We then suggest repeating and integrating ethical concepts in all subsequent business courses as described by the AACSB.

In the fourth part, we discuss other curricular elements such as interdisciplinary learning, multi-framing, leadership education, and civic engagement, using specific examples of how educators can implement these methods in the classroom. We end the book with a summary of recommendations for educators contemplating this approach. Following is a quick summary for each of the chapters, separated by parts.

Part 1: Theoretical Model for Professionalism and Prior Studies—Chapters 1 and 2

Chapter 1 briefly reviews the scholarly concepts associated with "professionalism" and the "profession," and argues the point of their relevance to today's education. This chapter points out that there is often limited use of these concepts, theoretical or in practice, in educational settings that teach management and other business disciplines. The goal is to point out the importance of a different curricular approach to teach this discipline in order to enhance the autonomy and social agency of pre-professionals, namely undergraduate business students.

Chapter 2 provides an understanding of the components of "professionalism" (Autonomy of Judgment, Expertise, Self-concept, and Social Agency) and the benefits of targeting these components pedagogically and in the classroom. It will briefly introduce the work that has been done in recent research studies on professionalism. Given that 68 percent of undergraduate students join professions at some point in their careers in areas such as business, engineering, health professions and others, this text proposes an educational approach that stresses these components.

Part 2: Wheel of Professionalism for Business Education Chapter 3

Chapter 3 provides a framework to build elements of professionalism within a professional program—in our case, business administration. This framework was originally developed by Miller (1985) for nursing, but adapted for business professionals in this study. Curricular elements of professionalism include a foundation of ethics, theory development, multi-frame and critical thinking, research and continuous knowledge building, community service orientation, code of ethics, participation in professional organizations, and autonomy. These areas need to be addressed in business programs to move them closer to professional programs. Each of these elements will be explained in the chapter. Thus, Chapter 3 lays the foundation for future chapters.

Part 3: Foundation of Ethics and Repeating Themes in Business Curriculum—Chapters 4 and 5

Chapter 4 discusses an issue that business schools have debated for years, namely, whether to offer a single course on business ethics versus integrating ethics within the entire business curriculum. We strongly propose a foundational business ethics course that allows students to become familiar with ethics as a discipline. The course should provide students with the framework and methodology for thinking of ethical dilemmas, regardless if they are associated with business or nonbusiness situations.

Chapter 5 argues that after building a foundation in ethics, it is important that students continue to see ethical issues in other business courses. As suggested by AACSB, we propose weaving ethical themes into all business curricula using a sequenced ethical model. Specifically, this means more attention to the stimulation of ethical sensitivity and motivation in the classroom, prior to ethical action. This step allows students to feel the ethical dilemmas first, prior to judging the rights and wrongs, and thus moving away from decisions that are based only on case facts and the law. Using Fink's (2013) Model "Taxonomy of Significant Learning" is consistent with this approach. This method invites students to consider ethical situations by looking deeply into the circumstances, using multi-framing and visualization, putting oneself into the situation, and understanding various societal views on an issue. We borrow from the literature that Gentile developed in *Giving Voice to Values* (GVV) and how her research tremendously helps in the development of professionals. This innovative curriculum allows professionals to express their autonomy and voice their values. The chapter covers the linkage between GVV and professionalism. The chapter also explains our recommended step approach of developing students by giving them a foundation in ethics, building their ability for ethical sensitivity, using the humanities to develop their professional identity, connecting students to their communities in order to grow their social agency—all of which support their abilities to express their thoughts and values.

Part 4: Suggested Curricular Path Towards Professionalism: Interdisciplinary Approaches for Theory Building, Multi-frame Thinking, Research and Knowledge Building, Leadership, Autonomy and Social Agency—Chapters 6, 7, and 8

Chapter 6 describes the use of multi-disciplinarily approaches as a method to integrate theory and multi-frame thinking into the business curriculum. We also show how simple interdisciplinary modules can assist business students develop critical thinking skills—business faculty working with faculty in the humanities, arts, and social sciences (and some in science), which are then integrated into one's business course. Faculty may also incorporate modules of global, environmental, and cross-cultural issues into an international business or marketing course. Moreover, for educational institutions that use paired courses, blocks, and the like, a course taught by business faculty can be linked to one taught by a faculty member in the humanities or sciences. These creative approaches also help build multi-frame thinking, ethical sensitivity, and autonomy in business students.

Chapter 7 examines the extensive literature on leadership and ties it to helping students develop the self-concept they need to become strong, autonomous professionals. The chapter starts by discussing that leadership and professionalism overlap and how both are critical to the development of business managers. By studying examples from the leadership literature, students begin to understand the different theories about leadership, thus encouraging critical thinking. The coursework described includes several assessments, which students can use to better understand their leadership skill and preferences. Use of these assessments helps students to look into themselves, which in turn can influence one's self-concept. The goal of the chapter is to allow students to focus on aspects of leadership that help them become better business managers and professionals.

Chapter 8 provides an applied methodology that helps business students develop social agency (an area based on the quantitative studies shows they are clearly lacking). The chapter utilizes approaches present in business schools such as international courses, but broadens the purpose of them to include societal components such as the influence of business growth on society. Additionally, the chapter incorporates new methods in service learning courses that allow students to make sense of their communities while learning how to use their professional expertise.

Summary and Recommendations—Chapter 9

Chapter 9 provides some ideas and advice regarding how to work toward a business curriculum that addresses the elements of professionalism, and especially social agency and ethical behavior. Building on the work of Colby et al. (2011), we provide additional recommendations about what can be done and how to implement the professional model. Reviewing trends in higher education, such as the evolution of online learning and the deep specialization of business faculty into separate disciplines (e.g., marketing, accounting, finance), we see many challenges and opportunities for change.

Acknowledgments

This book would not have been possible without the encouragement and participation of many people, including colleagues, students, and families. Its seeds were in Lana Nino's doctoral dissertation, which revealed the gaps in certain elements of professionalism among undergraduate business majors. Around the same time, the Andrew W. Mellon Foundation was interested in similar questions and invited colleges to apply for a grant to examine ways to integrate the humanities into undergraduate business programs. Strong support from Sharon Herzberger, President of Whittier College, as well as from faculty members in Business Administration, and colleagues in the arts, humanities, and social and natural sciences resulted in our receiving generous support from Mellon.

Although Whittier College has a long history of interdisciplinary collaboration, our work was made far more successful because of the generous funding from the Andrew W. Mellon Foundation. Indeed, they have committed to funding a similar project for the coming years. Needless to say, their vision about and commitment to the importance of integrating the liberal arts into professional programs has encouraged our business faculty in so many ways, and they in turn have encouraged us; so we thank them: Jeff Decker, Daniel Duran, and especially to our newer colleagues Fatos Radoniqi and Kristen Smirnov, who entered these waters prior to tenure!

Many, many thanks also goes to all those who helped develop the modules, pairs, and ideas for readings, films, and the like that could provide a different kind of case study: John Bak, David Bourgaize, Jonathon Burton, Michelle Chihara, Cinzia Fissore, Luz Maria Galbraith, Gil Gonzalez, Irfana Hashmi, Jennifer Holmes, Devin Iimoto, Paul Kjellberg, Ted Knoll, Mike McBride, Laura McEnaney, Sean Morris, Nat Zappia. And thanks to all of them for giving permission to include their work in the book.

And we especially thank our departments' secretaries, Maureen Nerio and Olivia Solis, as well as our student workers, Stacy Yamasaki and

Andrea Quiroz who helped us through research and the challenges of endnotes, different graphs, merging documents, and the like. Our sincere thanks to others behind the scene, particularly John Bak and Lisa Newton from the Office of Advancement, and Darrin Good, Vice President for Academic Affairs and Dean of Faculty.

The work of all those mentioned above and the vision and commitment of the Andrew W. Mellon Foundation were especially influential in Lana's and Susan's decision to take on the project of this book. We hope it can help other faculty who teach in undergraduate business programs.

We are also very thankful for the advice given by colleagues beyond Whittier College. Both Lana and Susan have benefitted from the Connective Leadership Institute, and from follow-up discussions with its director/author Jean Lipman-Blumen. Mary Gentile visited our campus and encouraged us to submit a prospectus for the book. And she has continued to encourage us through the process, including both suggestions and praise for the draft of the book. Craig Johnson also read the draft and provided ideas and encouragement. Finally, we both want to thank Ron Thomson for the editing that he did on the manuscript. As a writer who knows how to get to the core of issues, he was incredibly helpful.

Finally, there is also absolutely no question that this book came to fruition because of the support of family. Therefore, we offer a dedication to our families: From Susan to Ron and Jessica Jin Hwa Thomson: your encouragement and conversations were essential. It was a journey supported by my colleague Lana, from whom I learned so much. Additional dedications go from Lana to Sam, Tanya and her family, and Jason, for their encouragement and support for the project. A final important acknowledgment goes from Lana to her co-author, Susan D. Gotsch, former Dean of Faculty, for her willingness to join in the project, her belief in the cause, her work with business faculty and other faculty campus-wide, and for her dedication through the ups and downs of the writing of the manuscript.

PART 1

Theoretical Models of Professionalism and Prior Studies

CHAPTER 1

Reframing Professionalism as a Foundation for Business Education

There is much talk about the need for more social consciousness in the engineer, the scientist, and the doctor. Rarely do we see an analysis of why those professionals are not more socially conscious in the first place.

—Schein and Kommers[1]

Keywords

Business education, higher education, professionalism, precursors of professionalism, academic capitalism, autonomy, expertise, self-concept, social agency

Introduction

Despite much exploration into business education, the discipline may need an overhaul when it comes to graduating students who will be socially responsible managers in the work place. In spite of the efforts by business schools that emphasize ethical practices across all business disciplines, numerous studies show that business students continue to graduate with deficient knowledge when it comes to their role and responsibility in society as business managers.

Arguably, business education is more important than ever in US higher education. Business education is the largest group of undergraduate majors, constituting more than 20 percent of students in four-year institutions, year after year.[2] Higher education has many important public purposes, including the education of citizens for their participation in democracy.[3] The importance of business education stems from the centrality of business in society. The considerable number of undergraduates who select business for their field of study, and the even greater number who will be employed in business for their entire career, require higher education that will do more than just help students develop technical expertise. Advancing students' expertise in their chosen field or discipline is an important goal, but business education needs to do more to ensure that students understand their responsibilities as professionals and their influence on society. These preprofessionals must be able to connect their future role in business to the larger world. Business programs can attain these goals by changing their curriculum, and socializing and educating their faculty to teach professional concepts to students during their undergraduate education. Before we jump into the curricular approaches, we first must explain key elements that have influenced the discipline.

History of Business Education and the Need for a New Framework

At the start of the 20th century, when business education entered higher education, it had evolved from industry procedures and practices that were formalized as business theory and textbooks.[4] By the late fifties, business education had become a major component of American higher education, and two major research reports—the Pierson study and the Gordon and Howell report—examined the status of the discipline.[5] The reports advocated for rigorous curricular content in business school courses, the integration of liberal arts courses, and additional academic training of business faculty to bring them up to the level of other university faculty.[6] However, the high demand for business schools to produce an increasing number of graduates set the conditions that allowed these programs to continue using the same methods that were known weaknesses. The educators in business schools were composed of faculty from primarily professional tracks, which substantially influenced the instruction in the classes.[7] Given the qualifications and training of the faculty, greater emphasis was placed on teaching the students applied skills over theoretical knowledge, critical thinking, and the integration of theory into practice.

The quality of business schools influenced the courses offered to business students, increasing the emphasis on applied skills while decreasing the attention given to professional training. Khurana indicated that business schools proliferated during a time when there were numerous unresolved questions about the role of business and corporations in society, as well as uncertainty about their willingness to comply with broader societal objectives.[8] Khurana suspected that the change in business schools' focus on professional education occurred subsequent to the publication of Milton Friedman's doctrine on "business."[9] According to Khurana, Friedman's doctrine argued that the primary concern of US business should be the maximization of corporate profit and shareholder value, since any other system in his view would become a battleground for the conflicting interests of stakeholders.[10] This conflicting arrangement of varying interests would damage corporations and subsequently the economic well-being of society. The impact of this framework reached beyond the policies governing educational practices of the day by shifting attention toward the interests of economic policy, businesses, and stakeholders in the market. This framework also provided business managers with the justification to place the interest of the institutions first, without balancing the other interests of society with business practices and policies.[11] As this doctrine permeated the academic field of business, it became the prevailing theory that business schools used to guide business school practices, beginning at the University of Chicago, one of the most prominent business schools of the day.[12]

The doctrine advanced by Friedman had a major influence on business students and managers' indoctrination, thinking, and practice in the business world. The failure-to-success ratio in business in the United States has suggested that business students did not fully understand the influence of this doctrine on their business decisions and society.[13] Several studies revealed that students vacillate between business values learned in their programs—that emphasize the maximization of shareholders' wealth—and societal values, which require a balance between the needs of all stakeholders and society.[14] As Ehrensal noted, instead of an emphasis on pluralism and cultural sensitivity, the business curricula shifted toward competitiveness, which encourages students to have a competitive mentality and a primary goal of outperforming everyone with little, to no sensitivity regarding the costs incurred by others.[15]

These historical influences on business education highlighted important trends that influence the curricula and instructional practice in business schools.[16] Their effects have continued to impact practices in business education and can be observed at many business schools today. Yet, there were other influences on the business discipline, which we enumerate below.

Practical Knowledge Emphasis in Business Education

The success of business enterprises in the 20th century helped to fuel the growth of business schools.[17] During the onset of the globalization of the economy on a large scale, the commercial sector pressured the states, as well as the corporate sector, to introduce educational programs that would fill the demand for a commercial labor force that could compete in a global marketplace. This encouraged institutions to direct their efforts to the development of programs that fulfilled the needs of the market.[18] The close ties between business concerns and academia resulted in business schools' emphasis on the experiential aspects of business education over general education and the values of the business profession.[19] As industries demanded more practitioners' knowledge, business schools increased the emphasis on specialized skills in areas such as marketing, accounting, and finance.[20]

A consequence of the demand on practitioners' knowledge resulted in significant changes in the workforce. The percentage of adjunct and professional faculty who worked in business education has consistently remained above 51 percent of the total instructional workforce, an indicator of weak instruction. Of the adjunct and professional educator population, only 11 percent held Doctoral degrees, while the majority taught with only a Master's degree.[21] This teaching workforce, that lacked training in research, influenced business students' development of professional values in a manner that was not consistent with other undergraduate programs of study.[22] In fact, a bachelor in business administration degree rarely requires a research-methods course or a capstone with a research component.

However, the emphasis of business schools on experiential knowledge resulted in higher salaries for students, since this knowledge was responsive to corporate needs. The approach satisfied the desires of both students and business schools. The minimum requirements for a business degree identified by the market were met, which led to complacency in business schools concerning the need to improve the educational standards. Many scholars sought to explore this and in 1983, Hugstad studied business schools' offerings as compared to industry's preferences. He aimed to verify whether the industry still preferred practical training to analytical/theoretical training, and whether the attitudes of academicians and industry executives displayed any evidence of convergence. Hugstad surveyed 125 personnel directors, 250 deans of liberal arts schools, and 125 deans of business schools. He found that business personnel directors displayed continued indifference to the inclusion of the liberal arts training in business programs. The preference of businesses for applied skills and its influence on the curricula of business schools was a significant contributing factor to the lack of emphasis on the liberal arts in business schools.[23] The result was a myopic training paradigm. These training practices facilitated the development of expertise in students, at the expense of the other domains of the knowledge that business professionals needed to possess in order to develop as professionals. The influence of practical knowledge is a strong factor, but there have been and continue to be, other influences on business education.

Powerful Contemporary Influences on Business Education

Colleges and universities developed as nonprofit organizations that mainly relied on federal and state funding.[24] When state and federal funding decreased, these institutions restructured their programs to depend on other sources of funding. Slaughter and Leslie called this phenomenon "academic capitalism."[25] They described the relationship between academia and industry as organized networks that mediated between public and private sectors and utilized academic knowledge in a capitalistic form.[26] In these networks, organizations brought different sectors from industry and academia to address common problems that belonged solely to academia. For example, in 1980, corporations and legislators worked together to create individual education accounts (IEAs). The IEAs allowed workers to make tax-free contributions to savings accounts that workers could later use to retrain themselves in professional tracks or special certifications at colleges and universities offering to develop these specialized programs.[27] The network of businesses and universities redrew educational boundaries to take advantage of the new markets that were served by the new economy.

Donations to business schools did not stop and often corporations made generous contributions to business programs. One study estimated that there were 14 major donations to US business schools between 1997 and 2003, ranging from $23 million to $100 million.[28] These contributions were likely to have influenced the ideology of faculty and administrators at these campuses by encouraging them to customize educational offerings as if it were a "private good." Slaughter and Rhoades described this phenomenon by saying that the public, the faculty, the students, the corporations, and the state were "actors" rather than passive bystanders in this network that generated social changes.[29] The power of this network resided in academic capitalism, which blurred the boundaries between the private and public sector and allowed significant influence from the private sector on education.

In summary, business schools, with their tight connections to the business field, were a prime example of the application of the theory of "Academic Capitalism".[30] They taught management principles that helped corporations, but not society at large.[31] Thus, these institutions taught business principles that served the power of the corporation and its shareholders, rather than its societal stakeholders, in order to ensure the survival of their institution.[32]

Accreditation Organizations

Another influence on business education has been the main accrediting agencies for business programs in the United States, namely, AACSB (The Association to Advance Collegiate Schools of Business) and ACBSP (The Association of Collegiate Business Schools and Programs). These associations have the most authoritative power to dictate requirements at business schools. While both the major business-accrediting bodies (AACSB and ACBSP) have included business ethics in their accreditation requirements, neither has prescribed how business ethics is supposed to be included in the undergraduate business curriculum. This lack of specificity has led to inconsistent practices amongst business programs, thus leaving business students weakly prepared for the challenges of professional and ethical conundrums.[33] In addition, the AACSB often remained silent in response to the growing number of corporate financial scandals affecting the United States. In 2003, the AACSB made a recommendation that all business school curricula include content covering ethical practices as a requirement for accreditation, without recommending how to integrate into various courses.[34] As a result, the coverage of professional ethics in business coursework was inconsistent and often superficial.[35] Deans from business schools claimed that ethics and professional training were integrated in several courses, such as marketing, finance, operations management, accounting, and strategic management. However, this still failed to address the primary concern of including content specifically focused on ethical development, reflection, and practices. Swanson identified a large number of business professors who found it burdensome to include well-developed case points on ethics.[36] Swanson further explained that the professors rationalized their decision based on the desire to cover the required material in the courses and the lack of training to teach these concepts effectively. Not dealing with issues of ethical behavior likely influences the moral development of business students. These influencing factors may have weakened professional skills in business students in various ways.

Viewing Business Education Using the Lens of the "Profession"

Much research and discussion have taken place in the last few decades analyzing professions and professional theory. Most emphasized the special character of the knowledge and skill of the profession, in addition to the special ethical and altruistic orientation toward their clients. The term "Professionalism" used in this study refers to the important factors of professional identity including ethics—the norms of behavior within the framework of Rawls' behavioral duties.[37] Educational institutions and members of the profession are obligated to provide the training and socialization of these norms of ethical behavior to students who are new entrants to a profession.[38]

Nearly all of the definitions dealing with professionalism reference the key word "profession." Most scholars identify with Moore and Rosenblum's definition that a profession involves (a) a full-time occupation; (b) a sense of calling or commitment to the field; (c) a formalized organization; (d) esoteric, useful knowledge and skills based upon specialized training or education of exceptional duration and difficulty; and (e) an autonomy restrained by responsibility.[39] Scholars studying professions assume that common characteristics among professionals exist. These include (a) expertise that all professionals develop through rigorous training in higher education; (b) a sense of duty to the public good or the "social-trustee" element that compels individuals to restrain from actions of self-interest; and (c) autonomy in actions which stems from professional responsibility or the practice of independent judgment guided by special knowledge.[40]

Imse's work on the professionalization of business management encompassed the aforementioned qualities of professionalism. His work outlined the components of a profession as (a) fund of specialized knowledge; (b) a highly trained membership (intellectual training); (c) a code of ethics; (d) a sense of altruism; and (e) self-organization.[41]

Other scholars studying "professionals" added another category to the professionalism framework that they called "self-concept".[42] This category predicted readiness for carrying out the responsibilities of a professional role and captured survey participants' self-confidence in the practice of their profession. For example, a study of nursing professionals measured nurses' professional self-concept as they graduate and enter the profession. The items tested within the "self-concept" category included self-confidence stemming from expertise, communication ability, leadership, and interpersonal relationships.[43]

The previous categories of professionalism are appropriate as a framework for business education. Instead of focusing only on the ethical attitudes of business students, this book uses a comprehensive model of professionalism to capture a more robust education of professionalism beliefs. Using a comprehensive model of professionalism is also more consistent with other literature on professionalism, which considers more than ethical attitudes.[44] Factors such as "autonomy of judgment" and "self-concept" are critical to enable professionals to perform at higher levels when serving their clients and society.[45] For example, professionals who have high "self-concept" will be more likely to defend their position in a situation of ethical conflict in the workplace. Also, professionals exert their "autonomy of judgment" skills to express their professional opinions and avoid compromising external influences.[46] Strengthening all of the professionalism components is a necessary requirement to reach higher levels of performance and effectiveness for professionals.[47] This is especially important for the education of students who will enter the business world.

Current State of Professionalism

In addition to the components of professionalism described above, several scholars discussed the influence of the industrial revolution and the growth of a market economy on professionals and their behavior within organizations.[48] In essence, they examined the influence of capitalism on professionals. Identified were economic and political pressures that influenced professionals to deviate from the ideal type described above.[49] These influences allowed professionals to favor elements of professionalism, such as expertise, that draw financial rewards from the marketplace. The emphasis on knowledge and expertise had stronger ties to employment than the social-trustee beliefs that compel professionals to practice their profession while working toward the good of the public.[50] Furthermore, Brint noted that professionals wanted to shake free from precapitalist ideals of professionals respecting their "social-trustee" duties.[51] These duties compelled members within the profession to view themselves as aggregations of socially significant functions that work on a single important sphere of social life, such as health, education, and business.[52] However, professionals in those spheres had responsibilities beyond technical expertise, since they served as moral custodians of knowledge and its function as to how it served the public.[53]

Other scholars have discussed how the organizational structure of professions diminished the power of the professionals within that structure.[54] Influences of capitalism and the focus on generating profits within organizations changed their understanding of professionalism and limited the likelihood of hiring professionals who were interested in serving the public good.

Yet, higher education principles should have prevented economic, political, and structural factors to influence students' education pursuing professional tracks. Khurana stated that when graduate business education started in the late 19th century, it had the promise of developing graduates as professionals similar to disciplines such as law or medicine.[55] Additionally, Drucker stressed that business schools should view themselves as social institutions and not intellectual ones.[56] Social institutions have social missions rather than be merely developers of expertise. He expressed disappointment in the direction of business schools becoming more scientific in their applications of business methods, rather than becoming socially relevant.[57] Nevertheless, business schools started to align themselves with market organizations, thus training these graduates to fulfill the needs of the market.

Recent discussions about professions have centered on the deficiencies in the performance of professions. The activities of professionals have favored the pursuit of economic interest rather than the common good. Yet, professionals are still recognized as honored servants of public need due to their schooled application of unusually complex knowledge and skill. However, the main change is the growing trend for professionals to be employed in corporations, rather than self-employment as traditionally described for professionals. Employment is an important issue since it implies that the employer—rather than the professional—has the capacity to control work and how it is done, as well as the aim or goal of work. With professionals reporting to superiors in the workplace, literature in the professions reported a marked loss in autonomy, especially due to professionals' dependence on the dominant powers for their protection, namely job security and compensation.[58] Due to this constraint, professionals may become merely a part of the process rather than leading it.[59] The end result could be some loss of autonomy, which is a chief characteristic of a professional.

This book advocates educating business undergraduates and graduates using a comprehensive platform of professionalism and nurturing qualities such as autonomy and social agency, understanding that these preprofessionals—since they have not joined their professions—may have to function in a bureaucracy and need to maintain their autonomous thinking and behavior as professionals. In later chapters, we share classroom examples of how to nurture students' critical thinking skills in order to stimulate autonomous thinking in these preprofessionals. Additionally, we share other techniques focusing on societal issues that allow business students to connect with their communities, thus further developing students' interest in public good as intended in characteristics of professionals.

In this regard, this research relies on a framework of professionalism as defined by scholars who examined elements unique to professionals that enabled them to exert influential powers in their profession and society.[60] This framework highlights characteristics such as *"expertise," "autonomy," "self-concept," and "social agency"* that allow professionals to function in society as part of a social fabric, rather than as disconnected experts.[61] This book advocates an academic approach to classroom education that compels business faculty to become cognizant of professional theory and mechanisms as they educate in the classroom. Business is considered a professional track, and when it is combined with other professional majors, such as engineering, nursing, education, agriculture, and others, the total rises to 68 percent of all undergraduates.[62] Considering this large percentage of undergraduates who will practice as professionals in their future careers and considering their influence on society, the call to emphasize professional characteristics in the classroom is urgent.

Notes

1. Schein and Kommers (1972), p. 7
2. Snyder, Dillow, and Hoffman (2009).
3. Tierney (1989).
4. Foundation (1959); Pierson (1959); Porter and McKibbon (1988).
5. Gordon and Howell (1959).
6. Hugstad (1983); Pierson (1959); Porter and McKibbon (1988).
7. Khurana (2007); Martensson, Bild, and Nilsson (2008).
8. Khurana (2007).
9. Friedman (1970).
10. Khurana (2007).
11. Augier and March (2011); Khurana (2007).
12. Augier and March (2011); Khurana (2007).

13. Augier and March (2011); Khurana (2007); Nino (2011).
14. Augier and March (2011); Browning (2003); Khurana (2007); Swanson (2004); Swanson and Frederick (2001, 2003).
15. Ehrensal (2001).
16. Augier and March (2011); Khurana (2007); Swanson and Fisher (2009).
17. Pierson (1959).
18. Slaughter and Leslie (1997).
19. Brint (1996); Khurana (2007).
20. Porter and McKibbon (1988).
21. Cataldi, Bradburn, Fahimi, and Zimbler (2004).
22. Cataldi, Bradburn, Fahimi, and Zimbler (2004); Gordon and Howell (1959).
23. Porter and McKibbon (1988).
24. Slaughter and Leslie (1997); Slaughter and Rhoades (2004).
25. Slaughter and Leslie (1997);
26. Slaughter and Rhoades (2004).
27. Slaughter and Rhoades (2004).
28. Starkey and Tiratsoo (2007).
29. Slaughter and Rhoades (2004).
30. Slaughter and Leslie (1997).
31. Browning (2003); Parks (2005).
32. Augier and March (2011); Khurana (2007); Swanson and Fisher (2009).
33. Swanson and Frederick (2003); Trank and Rynes (2003).
34. Miles, Hazeldine, and Munilla (2004).
35. Miles, Hazeldine, and Munilla (2004); Swanson and Frederick (2001).
36. Swanson (2004).
37. Rawls (1999).
38. Kohlberg (1975); Pascarella and Terenzini (1991).
39. Moore and Rosenblum (1970).
40. Brint (1996); Freidson (1984); Goode (1957); Moore and Rosenblum (1970).
41. Imse (1962)
42. Arthur (1995); Freidson (1984); Haywood-Farmer and Stuart (1990).
43. Hensel (2009).
44. Freidson (2001); Hall (1968).
45. Freidson (2001).

46. Freidson (1984); Hall (1968).
47. Hall (1968); Imse (1962).
48. Brint (1996); Freidson (2001); Krause (1999).
49. Brint (1996); Freidson (1984).
50. Brint (1996); Freidson (1994).
51. Brint (1996).
52. Brint (1996).
53. Freidson (1984).
54. Krause (1999).
55. Khurana (2007).
56. Drucker (1968).
57. Drucker (1992).
58. Schein and Kommers (1972)
59. Freidson (1994).
60. Freidson (2001); Imse (1962).
61. Brint (1996); Freidson (2001); Imse (1962).
62. Colby, Ehrlich, Sullivan, and Dolle (2011); National Center for Educational Statistics (2010); Cowin (2001); Hall (1968); Haywood-Farmer and Stuart (1990); Imse (1962).

CHAPTER 2

Components of the Professionalism Model

. . . Professions show a pronounced . . . movement toward the rise of marketable expertise as a more or less exclusively important status element . . . The movement can be described as a movement from "social-trustee professionalism" to "expert professionalism" . . .

—Steven Brint[1]

Keywords

Business education, higher education, professionalism, precursors of professionalism, academic capitalism, autonomy, expertise, self-concept, social agency

Introduction

Scholars recognize the need to educate business students as future professionals in society. Brint, Friedson, and Khurana all advocated a tier of professionals who can become an informed force that can thwart government bureaucracy, narrow the gap between capitalists and labor, and advance society as a whole. Professionals are supposed to be guardians of knowledge, while serving societal goals and interests.[2] Friedson describes the ideal type of professional training by stating that:

> Professional training . . . is not merely practical in substance. Above all, the ideology supporting professional training emphasizes theory and abstract concepts . . . . Whatever practitioners must do at work may require extensive exercise of discretionary

judgment rather than . . . routine application . . . of mechanical techniques.[3]

The institutional focus on teaching professional expertise to students may have contributed to professionals becoming mechanical participants in their professional jobs. The aim of this book is to help develop professionals who are able to engage in business institutions by providing their knowledge, and yet be able to question authority, exercise autonomous judgment, understand broader societal goals, and perform their jobs as professionals without sacrificing their professional identity.

Prior Studies on Professionalism

In order to understand how to educate business students within a model of professionalism, we explore a number of prior studies. These studies, which include a number of professions, show that professional characteristics can be statistically measured in ways that signify strengths and weaknesses. Thus, we propose that colleges and universities, especially those with a business administration program, use the research and findings to target the weaknesses identified in preprofessional business students, and engage them in continuous professional development as part of the major.

Many of the scholarly works provide detailed definitions of the elements that have been used to define the professions. These include (a) belief in service to public; (b) belief in self-regulation; (c) sense of calling to the field; (d) feeling of autonomy; and (e) professional organizations as a source of authority (Figures. 2.1 and 2.2). Hall used a 50-item instrument

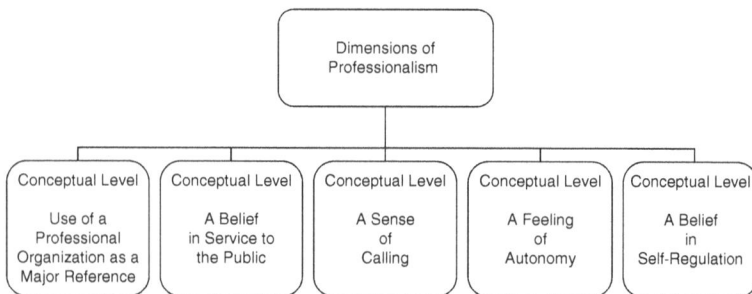

Figure 2.1 Professionalism Model (Hall Model)

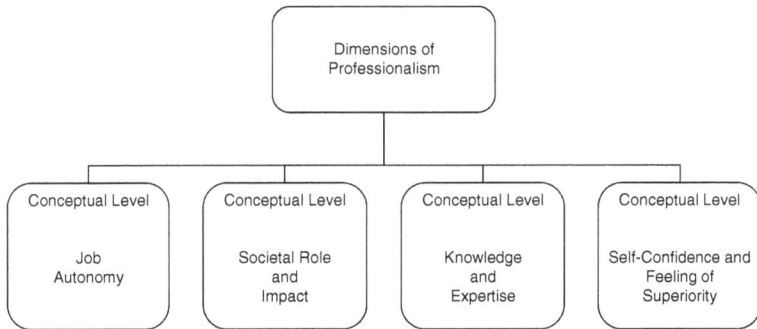

Figure 2.2 Professionalism Model (Haywood-Farmer and Stuart Model)

known as Hall's Professionalism Scale. He compared and ranked different professionals in accounting, advertising, law, engineering, medicine, business, and social work. Hall's studies focused on the structural and attitudinal facets of professionalization that influenced the strength of professional values. He wanted to assess whether there was a link between the strength of professional attitudes and socialization that took place in the work environment. Hall indicated an inverse relationship between bureaucratization and professionalism. An increase in bureaucracy in the workplace resulted in employees achieving lower scores on the professionalism scale. Hall attributed these results to employees' loss of autonomy due to the established hierarchy in the work environment that reduced employees' decision-making ability. This was an important finding due to the presence of a formal organizational structure in most businesses.[4]

Haywood-Farmer and Stuart's study examined professional values.[5] They developed an instrument to measure the degree of professionalism within medical services professionals (Figure 2.2). Haywood-Farmer and Stuart used an Exploratory Factor Analysis (EFA) to test an instrument that measured the following scales of professionalism: (a) job autonomy; (b) societal role and impact; (c) expertise; (d) self-confidence; and (e) feeling of superiority. They found that the dimensions generated by the full model were more useful to assess the degree of professionalism than individual components, such as expertise or autonomy.

Several professionalism studies conducted in the nursing profession examined the dimensions of nurses' general self-concept in connection with their profession.[6] Cowin used factor analysis to identify the following dimensions of professional self-concept: (a) a nurse's general self-esteem; (b) empathetic support given to another; (c) communications, defined as effectively sharing information and ideas; (d) knowledge using nursing skills and theories; (e) staff relations such as collegial relationships; and (f) leadership.[7] Most of these dimensions of "self-concept" were used again in Nino's study that is discussed below.

As mentioned above, several researchers studied professionalism in various fields. The prior studies highlighted the importance of studying the multi-faceted area of professionalism to better understand the dimensionality and factors that have influenced this latent attribute.[8] Additionally, the prior studies indicated that the scale of professionalism varied as a function of the organizational environment.[9] As Hall reported, the higher the bureaucracy in the organizational environment, the lower the professionalism factor-score.

The previous review of studies on professionalism guided Nino's study of senior-level business students and the precursors of professionalism they manifested. This study focuses on the *precursors of professionalism* for senior-level undergraduate students. The attitudes and values that students hold at the beginning of their work-life is likely to influence the type of professionals they become later in their careers.[10] The model in Figure 2.3 provides a lens to examine the promise of education—as scholars in education and ethics intended it—by exploring the professional

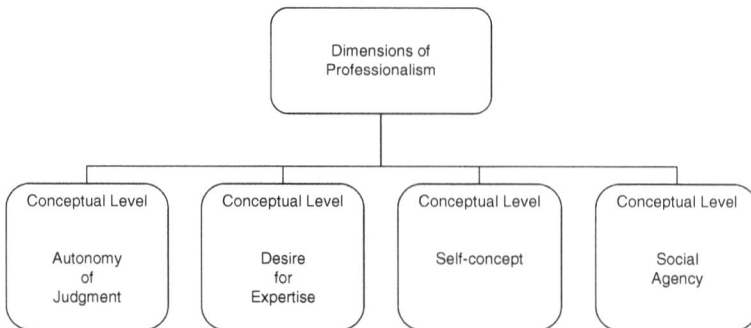

Figure 2.3 Professionalism Model (Nino Model)

attitudes of senior-level undergraduate students, immediately before they join the workforce.[11]

The conceptual basis for this study included the components of professionalism identified in prior research.[12] The graphic models for these studies, were presented before (see Figures. 2.1 to 2.3). The following are definitions of each element of the professional framework used in this study.

Autonomy of Judgment

Professional autonomy was defined as the practice of independent judgment guided by special knowledge.[13] The professional autonomy of the subjects was measured by their ability to make independent decisions given their expertise, with the guidance of professional associations.[14] This association provided the professionals with an authoritative source of reference for the rules and regulations of the profession.[15] Several scholars referred to the concept of professional autonomy in reference to many professions such as law, medicine, and accounting.[16]

Expertise

Expertise was determined to be a vital component of professionalism since it represents the foundational knowledge that justifies the reason for the profession.[17] Professional expertise was also found to be the core of professionals' economic assets that distinguishes them from other social classes.[18]

Self-concept

Arthur and Cowin suggested that "self-concept" was a key measure for professionalism since it is an attribute that professionals developed with their expertise in the profession.[19] It measured professionals' self-confidence in verbal, written expression, and leadership ability. The special knowledge that professionals attained provided them with a feeling of superiority over others.[20] Self-concept was also associated with higher intellectual and social self-concept ratings. [21]

Social-trustee

A foundational component of professionalism has been the strong ideological and ethical component that professionals developed.[22] Friedson defined this component as "claim a devotion to a transcendent value which infuses its specialization with a larger and putatively higher goal which may reach beyond that of those they are supposed to serve."[23] This definition which encompassed "a belief in service to the public" dictated that the work performed by the professional will benefit both the public and the practitioner.[24] This component was later renamed in Nino's study as "Social Agency" which is a term used by the Higher Education Research Institute at UCLA for essentially the same meaning of this category.

Another study on professionalism was done by the co-author of this book. In this recent study, Nino tested the "precursors of professionalism" of business students as specified in the prior literature. Nino employed the term "precursors of professionalism" since business students have not joined the profession, so the attributes only measured the "precursors" of these preprofessionals. To learn more about business students, this study used prior theoretical frameworks to model the precursors of professionalism— autonomy of judgment, desire for expertise, self-concept, and social agency. The study used data from the College Senior Survey (CSS) collected by the Higher Education Research Institute (HERI) at UCLA for two academic years from 2006 to 2008. Exploratory and confirmatory factor analysis indicated that the four factors—autonomy of judgment, desire for expertise, self-concept, and social agency—indeed fit a cohesive model for the latent construct "precursors of professionalism." The items that made up the four factors in this study are detailed in Table 2.1 below. The results of subsequent analysis of variance of the factor scores indicated that there are significant differences for most of the pairwise comparisons between business students and students from other majors. Below is a more detailed explanation of the results of the study.

Autonomy of Judgment Results

The results of the study show that business students, who comprise 17 percent of the sample, have higher factor scores than 43 percent of

Table 2.1 Measured Variables Used in This Study

Factor	Variables	Description	Scale
Autonomy	SLFCHG04	Change: Ability to think critically	1–5[a]
Autonomy	SLFCHG08	Change: Analytical and problem-solving skills	1–5[a]
Autonomy	SLFCHG17	Change: General knowledge	1–5[a]
Autonomy	SLFCHG19	Change: Knowledge of a particular field or discipline	1–5[a]
Autonomy	SLFCHG25	Change: Preparedness for employment after college	1–5[a]
Expertise	GOAL04	Goal: Become an authority in my field	1–4[b]
Expertise	GOAL10	Goal: Having administrative responsibility for the work of others	1–4[b]
Expertise	GOAL20	Goal: Obtain recognition from colleagues for my contributions	1–4[b]
Self-concept	RATE12	Self-rating: Leadership ability	1–5[c]
Self-concept	RATE18	Self-rating: Public speaking ability	1–5[c]
Self-concept	RATE22	Self-rating: Self-confidence (intellectual)	1–5[c]
Self-concept	RATE23	Self-rating: Self-confidence (social)	1–5[c]
Self-concept	RATE24	Self-rating: Self-understanding	1–5[c]
Social Agency	GOAL02	Goal: Becoming a community leader	1–4[b]
Social Agency	GOAL11	Goal: Helping others in difficulty	1–4[b]
Social Agency	GOAL12	Goal: Helping to promote racial understanding	1–4[b]
Social Agency	GOAL15	Goal: Influencing social values	1–4[b]
Social Agency	GOAL18	Goal: Keeping up to date with political affairs	1–4[b]
Social Agency	GOAL21	Goal: Participating in a community action program	1–4[b]

[a]1 = Much Weaker, 2 = Weaker, 3 = No Change, 4 = Stronger, 5 = Much Stronger

[b]1 = Not Important, 2 = Somewhat Important, 3 = Very Important, 4 = Essential

[c]1 = Lowest 10%, 2 = Below Average, 3 = Average, 4 = Above Average, 5 = Highest 10%

their peers in college, but lower than 40 percent of their other peers, after adjusting for gender and institutional differences. These scores of business students as a group are not significantly different from those who are non-business majors and a more sensitive test may need to be developed in this category in the future. Yet, based on the numerical ranking, this finding suggests that business education may need more emphasis on students' critical thinking skills, which may strengthen students' autonomy.

Desire for Expertise Results

The results of the study show that business students are the highest-ranking group—based on mean "desire for expertise" factor scores—among all majors after adjusting the marginal means for the covariates in the study. Additionally, scores of business students, as a group, are significantly different from nonbusiness majors. This finding suggests that business students are highly motivated to develop the business expertise necessary to enter their profession, especially since the profession offers high financial rewards for managers and executives working for corporations that are highly profitable .[25] Other scholars have discussed the hidden language in business education, emphasizing the corporate bottom-line and the success of managers in businesses.[26] This emphasis resulted in higher salaries for students, since this applied knowledge was responsive to corporate needs. These higher financial rewards may have caused business students to place high emphasis on attaining expertise in the profession.

Self-concept Results

The results show that business students who comprise 17 percent of the sample have higher factor scores than 74 percent of their peers in college, but lower than 9 percent of their other peers, after adjusting for gender and institutional covariates. Additionally, scores of business students, as a group, are significantly different from nonbusiness majors. This finding suggests that business education may have more emphasis on students' leadership abilities, which correlates to students' self-concept, as compared to most other majors. This was confirmed again by a study performed by the Graduate Management Admission Council (GMAC) of employers regarding their hiring practices that consisted of 1,509 participants representing 905 companies in 51 countries. Most employers reported that business students have higher abilities in motivation, and learning, when compared with other employees at the same job.[27]

Social Agency Results

The results of the study show that business students who comprise 17 percent of the sample score lower in their factor scores than 71 percent of their peers in college but higher than 12 percent of other peers in "social agency" scores, after adjusting for gender and institutional type. Additionally, scores of business students, as a group, are significantly different from nonbusiness majors. This finding suggests that business education has a lower emphasis on ethical and social issues in their education, as discussed by prior scholars.[28] Business students rank in the same grouping as technical majors—such as engineering, math, and physical sciences—in mean factor scores of social agency. This is another piece of evidence that students are being educated in a manner similar to those in technical fields, such as physicists, engineers, and others. The business curriculum's emphasis on accounting, finance, marketing, economics, and statistics does not leave much room for meaningful integration of other disciplines.[29] Although it continues to be necessary to provide technical training to business students, in order to meet corporate needs, it is highly urgent to recognize that business students become managers of organizations, where their decisions have societal consequences. Therefore, their future roles in business should influence the direction of their education.[30]

Institutional and Environmental Factors

It is likely that students who majored in business arrived at their college or university predisposed to a focus on developing expertise and had little interest in contributing to their community and society. Additionally, students' choice of major and the norms within the business departments where students enroll might, in turn, support and nurture their natural tendencies, thereby increasing the likelihood that business students will achieve the above results in their precursors of professionalism. Higher

Education scholars argue that academic environments can differentially reward and reinforce students' varying interests and abilities.[31]

> Some evidence suggests that academic majors differentially shape students' attitudes, interests, and abilities. Smart and his colleagues provide the most convincing evidence that academic environments differentially reward and reinforce different interests and abilities, accentuating initial differences. The changes in students' abilities and interests are greatest when students enter an academic environment congruent with their initial interests. (p. 326)

Business students may select the major based on their initial interest and abilities in the subject matter, but the major's academic environment can accentuate these initial differences in students. The results in the precursors of professionalism may have been due to students' initial interests in business expertise as well as their natural abilities in leadership; yet the academic environment that was congruent with students' interest may have accentuated the students' results.

In summary, the results of the study on precursors of professionalism show great promise in the development of business students' professional acumen or expertise, but also some deficiency in other areas of the professionalism scale such as autonomy and social agency. This result may influence decisions and actions of future business managers and their promise to develop fully as professionals. The implications of this study call for a more in-depth use of the professional framework in the education of business students.

Implications of the Study

The implications of the results in this study are important to business education and the business profession. Compared to their peers—especially those who are in other social science fields—business students score higher than most in the areas of their "desire for expertise" and "self-concept" and lower in "social agency." Students' results in "desire for expertise" and "self-concept" show great promise in the development of their skills toward professionalism. These students are excited about their fields of discipline as shown by their high scores in the "desire for expertise" factor. They also have confidence and strong self-concept to succeed in their field as shown by their scores in the "self-concept" factor. Yet, their lower scores in "social agency" reveal that business students may be deficient in their promise to develop as full professionals. As previously noted, this study did not examine the predictors that influence their scores, such as precollegiate individual characteristics, experiences, and programs students joined in college, internships, parental attitudes, economic status of students, academic ability, and a myriad of other factors that may influence these precursors.

Importantly, this study shows that students' major of study is a significant factor for students' scores, and that business students have low scores as compared to their peers in some areas related to professionalism. Moreover, Khurana, Swanson and Frederick, Trank and Rynes all point to the deficiencies in business education when it comes to integration of ethics and awareness of social issues within the business curriculum.[32] The theoretical framework on hidden curriculum, used in this study, may also explain business students' lower scores in "social agency." The overemphasis of the business curriculum on duties to shareholders rather than stakeholders may have influenced students' social agency. Colby et al. called for the overhaul of business education.[33] These scholars proposed strategies for curriculum, teaching methods, and program arrangements that can transform undergraduate business education into a discipline that graduates socially-conscious professionals. Additionally, Colby et al. explain that the goal of education is to develop and graduate students who have capabilities in the area of analytical reasoning, the ability and disposition to take multiple perspectives when confronting a complex decision or judgment, and the capacity to make connections of personal meaning between what one does and who one intends to become.[34] All of these characteristics allow students to develop a professional identity. This is likely where business education fails, namely, in the formation of a complete professional identity where students are able to integrate their expertise with autonomy and social responsibility.

New Directions for Business Education

Along the lines of Colby et al. in *"Rethinking Undergraduate Business Education,"* this book calls for integrative learning for students, which requires institutional intentionality.[35] This integrative learning suggests weaving liberal arts subjects with business subjects. The result does not occur by merely adding a humanities or science requirement to business.

This book calls for a set of courses and teaching methods that require students to make thoughtful, well-informed choices about their future in business and recognize how their business roles will affect the meaning of their lives and the kinds of people they become. The process we suggest conforms to Kohlberg's theoretical framework that is based on moral development through stages of maturation.[36] Doing so will support business students in their development of critical thinking and ethical evaluation modeling during the 4 years of college. Business programs should aim for students to develop a conceptual vocabulary for thinking and talking about ethical issues and choices. Having a series of business program courses that offer theoretical and integrated experiences certainly requires more than just distribution requirements within a program. The courses should build on one another and add up to a powerfully integrated student experience. Its design has an intentional structure to provide a sound and responsible business education.

This study on the "Precursors of Professionalism" confirms the need for all business programs to adopt an approach to business education that incorporates the professional view and highlights the influence of this profession on society. We argue that this book will help students develop a full professional identity that is embedded with responsibilities, as well as expertise. This study confirms that our business graduates echo the weaknesses identified by prior scholars. This confirmation points to the need to revamp our educational methods to weave professional approaches into our current curriculum and methods of education. We recommend that educators start by helping students assess their facets of professionalism. A simple questionnaire is included in Table 2.2. The questionnaire can be used in a simplified numerical scale allowing the students to compare their score of one section to the others, thus identifying their strengths and weaknesses.

In the next chapter, we review other professions that have taken the journey from occupation to a profession, including medical and nursing professions. Both Chitty and Black in the nursing field, and Wear and Bickell in medical education, have made significant contributions to their

Table 2.2 Classroom Instrument

		Rate yourself from 1 to 5 on the following items, and check scale below		Reverse
1	ASLF10	I value my colleagues' opinions more than my own in making a decision	1–5[b]	Yes
2	ASLF20	My family relies on my advice related to my discipline	1–5[a]	No
3	ASLF30	Others defer to me when making an important decision	1–5[a]	No
4	ASLF40	I tend to over-think situations from all sides	1–5[a]	No
5	ASLF50	My colleagues think through decisions more than I do	1–5[b]	Yes
6	EXSLF10	I respect my colleagues who are competent in their work	1–5[a]	No
7	EXSLF20	I enjoy developing others in my field	1–5[a]	No
8	EXSLF30	My colleagues respect my work	1–5[a]	No
9	EXSLF40	I aspire to keep up to date on new research in my field	1–5[a]	No
10	EXSLF50	I aspire to generate new knowledge in my field	1–5[a]	No
11	SRATE10	My friends have better public speaking ability	1–5[b]	Yes
12	SRATE20	Others compliment my communication ability	1–5[a]	No
13	SRATE30	My friends are more confident in leading groups than me	1–5[b]	Yes
14	SRATE40	I can improve in my communication ability	1–5[a]	Yes
15	SRATE50	I seek opportunities to show my leadership ability	1–5[a]	No
16	SAG10	I seek to understand social and political issues around me	1–5[a]	No
17	SAGJ20	I help my friends understand social and political issues	1–5[a]	No
18	SAGJ30	My peers participate in community initiatives more than me	1–5[b]	Yes
19	SAG40	My peers consider me a principled individual	1–5[a]	No
20	SAG50	I consider the consequences and reflect in all my decisions	1–5[a]	No

[a] 1 = Disagree, 2 = Weakly Agree, 3 = Somewhat Agree, 4 = Agree, 5 = Strongly Agree
[b] 5 = Disagree, 4 = Weakly Agree, 3 = Somewhat Agree, 2 = Agree, 1 = Strongly Agree

Scales	
Autonomy Scale, Item 1–5	
Expertise Scale, Item 6–10	
Self-concept Scale, Item 11–15	
Social Agency Scale, Item 16–20	

Scores	
90–100	Excellent
80–90	Very good
70–80	Average
Less than 70	Below average

fields in terms of professionalism.[37] We argue that all methods suggested in their writing and those we suggest should be implemented with an eye on the traditional characteristics of professionals: autonomy of judgment, expertise, self-concept, and social agency. Importantly, in Chapter 3, we outline the curricular approaches that allow colleges and universities to develop business students in these professional dimensions. These curricular approaches include:

- A foundation of ethics with repeating themes
- Theory development orientation
- Multi-framing, critical thinking, and leadership
- Research and continuous knowledge building
- Community service orientation
- Adherence to a code of ethics and standards
- Professional organization participation
- Self-regulation and autonomy

We adopted most of these elements from the prior literature about weaving professionalism into preprofessional education. We explain them in a practical, implementable context allowing individual business faculty or business departments or schools to adopt them. We see this implementation as a continuing journey, rather than one action plan. We also view that any improvement faculty members make toward the development of better professionals is an important improvement for the future of our society.

Notes

1. Brint (1996), p. 203.
2. Brint (1996); Freidson (2001); Khurana (2007).
3. Freidson (2001).
4. Hall (1968).
5. Haywood-Farmer and Stuart (1990).
6. Cowin (2001); Hensel (2009).
7. Cowin (2001).
8. Cowin (2001); Haywood-Farmer and Stuart (1990).
9. Hall (1968).

10. Nyström (2009).
11. Damon (2009); Kohlberg (1976); Pascarella and Terenzini (1991).
12. Cowin (2001); Hall (1968); Haywood-Farmer and Stuart (1990); Imse (1962).
13. Goode (1957); Moore and Rosenblum (1970).
14. Moore and Rosenblum (1970).
15. Freidson (1994).
16. Freidson (1984); Hall (1968).
17. Brint (1996); Freidson (1984).
18. MacDonald and Ritzer (1988).
19. Arthur (1995); Cowin (2001)
20. Haywood-Farmer and Stuart (1990).
21. Freidson (1984); MacDonald and Ritzer (1988).
22. Brint (1996).
23. Freidson (2001).
24. Goode (1957).
25. Crainer and Dearlove (1999); Khurana (2007).
26. Bowles and Gintis (1976).
27. General Management Aptitude Test (2011).
28. Khurana (2007); Swanson and Fisher (2009); Trank and Rynes (2003).
29. Bennis and O'Toole (2005); Khurana (2007).
30. Colby, Ehrlich, Sullivan, and Dolle (2011); Khurana (2007).
31. Terenzini and Pascarella (2005).
32. Swanson and Fredrick (2001); Khurana (2007); Trank and Rynes (2003).
33. Colby, Ehrlich, Sullivan, and Dolle (2011).
34. Colby, Ehrlich, Sullivan, and Dolle (2011).
35. Colby, Ehrlich, Sullivan, and Dolle (2011).
36. Kohlberg (1976).
37. Chitty and Black (2011); Wear and Bickel (2009).

PART 2

Wheel of Professionalism for Business Education

CHAPTER 3

Pathway to Professionalization for the Business Discipline

Expert knowledge, skill in its application, and an acquired identity
in which individual interest is subordinated to group norms revolving
around the service of a greater good—these three elements . . . virtually
constitute the institution we call the professions . . .

—Rakesh Khurana[1]

Keywords

Business education, higher education, profession, professionalism, professional socialization, autonomy, expertise, self-concept, social agency, multi-framing, foundation in ethics, critical thinking

Introduction

The role of business in society is poorly understood and can be quite complex due to the number of stakeholders involved in the cycle of business and the influence of the business operation on each of them. Decisions made by business managers cannot be linked easily to societal consequences. Additionally, the number of business managers and their responsibilities in society have grown tremendously. After industrialization and during the 20th century, many businesses expanded into huge, powerful, influential corporations, employing thousands of managers not necessarily trained for the responsibilities given to them.[2] Although these managers needed more professionalization than owners of small ventures, their education failed to emphasize professional development. Despite the fact that standardized codes of ethics exist for some business professionals—accountants and marketers, for example—there is not an accepted set of ethical standards for all business professionals. Additionally, there is no consensus on whether a business degree is a professional degree.[3]

Understandably, when students join business programs, they often are ambivalent about their professional identity.[4] Most *Introduction to Business* or *Business and Society* texts do not have a single chapter on how to become or what it means to be a business professional. That reality raises several questions. Is it time for business programs to commit to educating professionals with professional degrees? Who will take responsibility for socializing these students and helping them understand their role in society?

In the next few paragraphs, we will discuss how other professions made the transformation from occupational to professional education, and identify the elements needed to transform business programs.

Comparisons Between the Business Profession and Others

The business profession is unique in the professional path it has taken. Some disciplines within the business major, such as accounting, have taken a more accelerated road toward professionalism, while others lag behind. Some see no perceived immediate need to change.

In other professions such as nursing, law, and medicine, all stakeholders agree that professionals in these disciplines must portray and internalize all the elements of professional training, including a strong self-concept, autonomous judgment, social agency, as well as expertise. For instance, both clients and law firms expect attorneys to demonstrate expertise, be critical thinkers, be wise and have independent judgment, and care about client and company interests equally. More generally, society expects attorneys to be engaged members in the community, and adhere to all established laws.

Nursing provides a second example. A nurse working at a hospital, the employer in this case, fits easily into the professional model. In addition to adhering to all hospital's policies and caring about employer interest, nurses are expected to care about patients interests and professionally reconcile any conflicts. They must exercise good judgment under difficult circumstances and be able to weigh the risks and rewards of their decisions.

In both the law and the nursing models, it is easy to see a direct relationship between the professional and the client. In both cases, employers fully sponsor obligations to their clients. This obligation to the recipients of their services is a common criterion shared by all professionals.[5] Although there are similarities to the business profession and the clients it serves, there are notable differences.

For a business professional, whether it be a business manager, a marketing vice-president, or a sales manager, the duties owed to employer and clients are structured differently. Even if a business manager has loyalty to the employer and to the clients of the employer, the relationship between the manager and the clients is not as direct as in the other professions (Figure 3.1). In fact, corporate business managers may feel detached, assuming more responsibility to the company or employer than to its customers. This may change loyalties and professional duties. In a bureaucratic organization, the working relationship between the business manager and the employer may reduce professional autonomy.[6]

This reality underscores the need for business colleges to adopt a professional education model. In *Giving Voice to Values*, Gentile argues persuasively that managers need to learn how to negotiate their professional autonomy and balance customer and employer relationships. In a later chapter, we will discuss how her approach has been used extensively in business programs.[7]

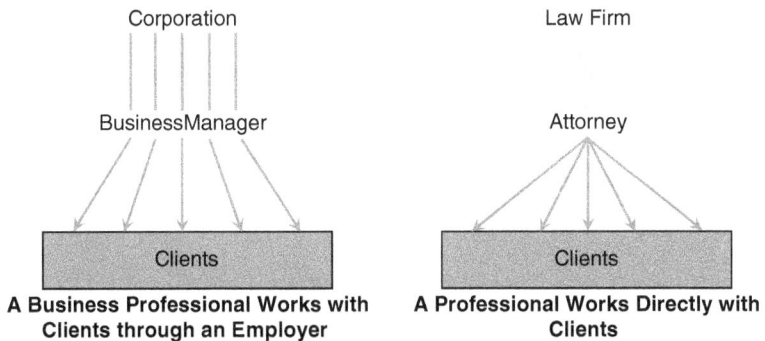

Figure 3.1 *Relationship between Professionals and Clients*

Another difference relates to the support that professional organizations give to their professional practitioners and the missions they lay out for members. Consider, for example, the American Bar Association (ABA). The ABA's first tenet for law graduates is to "understand their ethical responsibilities as representatives of clients, officers of the courts, and public citizens responsible for the quality and the availability of justice." The curricular content that the ABA outlines includes "understanding of the theory, philosophy, role, ramifications of the law and its institutions" in addition to skills and expertise needed for the practice.[8] These professional requirements provide a vision to the profession and professionals working within it, normalizing their behavior within society. Compare the ABA to the AACSB. Although the AACSB has facilitated the standardization and the accreditation of business programs, unlike the ABA, it has no curricular requirements for theory, philosophy, or a separate requirement for a foundational course on ethics.

An awareness of these comparisons should help business schools, professional organizations, and business faculty understand how adoption of a professional model can enrich business students' education and nurture their professional growth. In the next sections, we outline the theoretical models of student socialization toward professionalism and highlight the educational elements needed in these programs.

Steps for Professional Socialization in All Business Tracks

To educate students to become a professional is distinctly different from educating them for skills and expertise.[9] Educators must recognize that it is harder to turn undergraduates into professionals in 4 years than it is to grant them a business degree. We start by borrowing socialization models in nursing education that may be helpful in any professional field. Cohen outlined a socialization model that considers the different phases young professionals may go through on their journey to a profession.[10]

Cohen's Model of Professional Socialization

Cohen's model identifies four stages in professional socialization. These stages help explain the phases that students go through as they commit to their majors, start their experiences in the field, and later join in the workplace as professionals.[11]

- Unilateral dependence: Is the phase where students may show the most reliance on external authority and do limited critical analysis and questioning. As students take their early business courses, they are more apt to place a lot of trust in faculty and role models.
- Negativity/independence: With some experience in the field, students may show cognitive disagreement and diminished reliance on external authority.
- Dependence/mutuality: After a reasoned appraisal, students begin to integrate facts and opinions.
- Interdependence: Students arrive at a collaborative decision with commitment to the professional role, and begin to internalize a professional role identity.

Faculty who are aware of Cohen's model are in a better position to understand how student thinking matures. Students may join business programs predisposed to certain mental images of the business environment and the actors within it. While students are enrolled in the program, they probably will need to resolve conflicts regarding their beliefs and what faculty members are teaching. Understanding the phases to professionalism will help faculty observe student growth and recognize the steps they take to reach "dependence" and "interdependence."

In the next section, we define the criteria that a profession must meet, and outline educational elements that will help elevate a business program to a professional program.

Meeting the Criteria of a Profession

Several scholars have outlined the criteria that an occupation must meet to be classified as a profession.[12]

- A profession should have a well-organized body of specialized knowledge that is developed by the scientific method and targets intellectual levels of higher learning. A profession aspires to grow this body of knowledge continuously, through research and contributions of its professionals.

- Discipline is taught in higher education at educational institutions that teach the theory and practice of the profession to its members.
- This professional knowledge and its practical services are applied to human and social welfare where the knowledge of the profession helps advance society and facilitates the dynamics within it.
- Through its professional organizations, the profession works independently to formulate professional policies, which control and guide its professionals. This process helps achieve the autonomy of the profession and the professionals within it.
- Professionals aspire to grow, lead, and serve their profession in ways that are consistent with society's expectation. These professionals recognize their selected occupation as an important life's work and exalt service above personal gain.
- The profession has a recognizable code of ethics that practitioners recognize and follow. Additionally, the profession (association) supports high standards of service.

Need for a New Paradigm

A survey of current practice reveals that business meets some of these criteria including a recognizable body of knowledge taught at higher education institutions. This is particularly true in certain specializations and in advanced degree programs at the masters and the doctoral levels. There is considerable scientific research in the business field, a requirement for a profession,[13] and there have been advancements in formulating policies to guide professionals and achieve professional autonomy. Thousands of professionals have joined organizations such as the AACSB, the American Management Association (AMA), the American Marketing Association (AMA), the American Accounting Association (AAA), and the American Finance Association (AFA). These associations expect their professionals to "grow, lead, and service" their profession as described in the fifth criteria. Most of these organizations have adopted a code of ethics.

What about business education? Many colleges and universities offer degrees in business and consider them professional degrees. How do they measure up to the six criteria? More to the point, are these schools using a professional model to develop their students? In the next section, we will describe the educational elements of a business program focused on developing professionalism.

Educational Elements of a Professional Program

Business is not the first discipline to evolve from occupation to profession. Because nursing has already made the transition successfully, we use resources developed in that field to inform our ideas.[14] The "Wheel of Professionalism in Nursing," developed by Adam and Miller to visually conceptualize professionalism in nursing, can be adapted and applied to business by adding one new element—Multi-frame Critical Thinking and Leadership—and slightly modifying others.[15] One element from the Adam and Miller model—Publication and Communication—is incorporated in the Research and Continuous Knowledge Building element. Sequenced steps in this revised model show how students would experience them on their path to professionalism.

Along with a required "body of knowledge," here are the educational elements that move a business curriculum from occupation to profession.

- Foundation in ethics with repeating themes in all business courses
- Theory development orientation
- Multi-frame critical thinking and leadership
- Research and continuous knowledge building
- Community service orientation
- Adherence to a code of ethics and building standards
- Professional organization participation
- Self-regulation and autonomy

These elements are described in detail below and depicted in Figure 3.2.

Wheel of Professionalism

Figure 3.2 The Wheel of Professionalism for Business Students (Adapted from Miller, 1985).

Building a Foundation in Ethics

Preprofessional business students need a foundation for managing future complex ethical issues within their profession. During the education process, students will study the theoretical frameworks used to make ethical decisions. When these future professionals encounter ethical dilemmas, they will attain the skills to apply theory and decision-making models to real-world situations. They will learn to differentiate values, morals, ethical theories, and ethical principles and develop a decision-making process that fits into the context of their own value system. They will also be able to handle a variety of situations, rather than follow rules based on a fixed set of circumstances. The end result is for students to negotiate between their personal and professional ethics and apply the latter in work settings.

Ethical action includes several components: moral sensitivity, moral judgment, moral motivation, and moral action.[16] Students who understand these components will recognize an ethical dilemma when encountered. They will have learned what it means to use ethical sensitivity, apply moral judgment, have the courage to express their views once they reach moral motivation, and execute a moral action despite any hardships they may encounter.[17] This ethical foundation is necessary for professionals in any field, if they intend to act with autonomy and commitment in the workplace.

Theory Development

Theory is a powerful foundation for the continuous generation of knowledge.[18] Theory has many definitions, but it generally refers to concepts and definitions used to explain and predict outcomes. The ability to grasp what's happening in new and different situations is a powerful skill critical to professional success. Development of a theoretical foundation allows students to be nimble in changing business environments. As business knowledge evolves, it requires ongoing interaction between theory and practice. Some scholars argue that inter-disciplinary thinking adds an additional and critical element to generating an even richer body of business knowledge.[19] Theories drawn from disciplines—history, sociology, political science, and leadership—enrich business education, and enable graduates to relate to broader audiences and to adapt to different contexts. Mastery of theory improves the thinking skills, employability, and mobility of well-schooled business professionals.[20]

Multi-frame, Dialectical Framing, Critical Thinking, and Leadership

This educational element expands the autonomous thinking skills of students, as well as their social agency to society. It targets students' capacity to apply several interpretive frames to a situation or a case study. Dialectical framing allows students to see a situation from opposing sides, a skill that is often taught to attorneys. The more students are able to frame and reframe their thinking, the easier it becomes for them to negotiate today's complex professional life. This process is critical in developing students' autonomy of judgment as described in previous chapters. To help students master theoretical concepts allows them to appreciate ambiguity and find new ways to solve problems, rather than rely on the application of rules and formulas for solutions.[21] Teaching professional knowledge as an inquiry or study of implications advances critical thinking and develops students' abilities to generate knowledge rather than just apply it.

The leadership discipline offers opportunities to expand self-concept, autonomy, and social agency in preprofessionals, which is a topic we will explore in a later chapter. As students discover their personal style of leadership, they begin to focus on their strengths and what those strengths imply for their professional development. Leadership skills strengthen students' self-confidence and improve their abilities to start and lead projects, work in teams, and negotiate through professional conflicts.

Research and Continuous Knowledge Building

To continue the practice of quality knowledge building, professionals and their organizations must use a disciplined approach to add to the profession's body of knowledge. Scientific achievements should be used to ensure that new knowledge is built on sound principles and theory rather than simply creative ideas.[22] All research disciplines use an orderly, systematic way of thinking and solving problems. This scientific method applies to quantitative and qualitative techniques as well.[23]

New knowledge is an important component of a dynamic profession and this knowledge needs to be generated by the professionals and preprofessionals who commit to it. Research findings are different from practical knowledge. Research builds on a foundation of prior scientific findings, has theoretical frameworks, and is widely transferable. Practical knowledge is situation specific and cannot be generalized, as shown in Table 3.1. Therefore, a research component built into undergraduate business programs would help develop a culture of research and knowledge building amongst students or preprofessionals.[24]

Table 3.1 Difference Between Research and Problem Solving

Research	Problem Solving
• Research findings are widely experienced	• Problem solving is situation specific
• There is a theoretical framework for research problems. It is based on a foundation of literature, identifying latest research in the field	• Problem solving is based on practical knowledge, commonsense, and experience
• Findings are generalizable to a wide set of similar situations	• Only useful to the problem at hand and transferability must be examined

Adapted from Chitty and Black (2011), p. 259

Integrating business research into the curriculum requires a foundation in research, either qualitative or quantitative. Many college disciplines—history, economics, anthropology, and political science, for example—have integrated a research foundation course in their curriculum. Frequently, students use the research course to fulfill the capstone requirement for the major. In order for business to reach a higher level on its journey from occupation to profession, this model trend should be adopted for business education as well.

Community Service Orientation to Develop Social Agency

Business is a profession that promotes the economic well-being of its stake-holders, whether they are customers, suppliers, or communities.[25] This stake-holder theory of the firm states that businesses serve a broad public purpose: to create value for society.[26] Business is an essential activity in any society, and it should be practiced according to established professional standards.

A broad range of studies has shown that the success of business relies on executing business transactions in an equitable, fair, and transparent manner to all parties.[27] Business professionals aspire to provide this service while furthering their own economic well-being. No one questions the right of business professionals to charge reasonable fees or prices for their services and commodities. And the high salaries of some business professionals insure the continued attractiveness of the profession to those who might choose business as a career. Salary, however, should not impact the professionals' altruism or professionalism.[28] No matter the salary, professionals in society have a societal obligation to serve a higher purpose.[29]

Emphasizing the higher purpose of business to students helps stimulate their calling to the profession and their social agency. Table 3.2 shows how to present higher purpose to students, and is consistent with corporate social responsibility principles, as well as newer scholarship done by Mackey and Sisodia on conscious capitalism.[30] This approach permits students to think of their own purpose for selecting the profession and synchronize that with the higher purpose of business.

Using this grounding in the higher purpose of business provides incentives to students to serve in their communities and strengthens their

Table 3.2 Higher Purpose of Business

Business	Higher Purpose of Business
• Maximize shareholders' value	• Viewing shareholders, customers, suppliers, community, and the environment as key stakeholders in value maximization
• Create efficient and mutually beneficial relationships with customers (exchange concept)	• Create fair, transparent, and mutually beneficial partnerships with stakeholders
• Creating products for customers that are sold at a profit	• Creating quality, safe, and innovative products for customers that are sold at a price that balances the responsibility of business to investors and their stakeholders.
• Seeks to maximize business and political power in society	• Believes in balance of power of corporations in society

social agency. Because research suggests that business professionals have lower social agency and allegiance to society,[31] business schools have an opportunity to elevate their students' professional calling. As students graduate and become business managers with sizable responsibilities to their companies, if they are not educated fully in all facets of professionalism, they may fail in their duty to society.[32] To produce well-rounded professionals, many scholars have shown that the inclusion of civic engagement in degree programs will have a beneficial influence on the liberal learning of students.[33]

Adherence to a Code of Ethics and Standards in the Profession

Most of the early scholars who attempted to define professions mentioned ethical behavior as a hallmark.[34] A code of ethics is a list of statements that guide professionals toward a more salient self-definition with evidence of professional legitimacy. In business, a code of ethics establishes how a business operates within a social context and guides the interaction of all business professionals with their stakeholders.

As mentioned previously, business is a profession with many disciplines and underlying professions. When business students graduate, although no single code of ethics will govern their conduct, many professional organizations in accounting, management, and marketing have unique codes of ethics with some common provisions. Some business programs now have graduating students sign a code of ethics. Harvard Business School was one of those pioneers.

> "True professions have codes of conduct," wrote Harvard Business School (HBS) professors Nitin Nohria and Rakesh Khurana in a 2008 Harvard Business Review article:

> "At the end of Class Day exercises (June 3), approximately half of the 886 graduating HBS students took the professors' comments seriously enough to sign a managerial version of the Hippocratic oath, pledging to manage the companies they work for in a way that safeguards not just the interests of stakeholders, but of fellow employees, customers, and the larger society in which they function."[35]

Today's business environment often presents challenges to professional ethics. Wall Street and market pressures on companies, in addition to international competition, are a few of the factors that strain business practices. A code of ethics for all business professionals and preprofessionals is a step toward professionalization. While professional organizations may follow with standards within their own disciplines, a set of uniform principles in a code of ethics should guide all business professionals. Standards of practice should outline the competencies that professionals attain to become managers, marketers, or accountants.

Professional Organization Participation

Every profession needs an association that works to improve standards and practices.[36] These associations promote the professional development of their members and advance their autonomy and economic and general welfare. They encourage and support ethical standards of practice and are committed to the continuous improvement of the profession. Professionals should recognize the benefits of membership, which in turn encourages them to join.[37]

Presently, memberships in the different professional organizations such as the AMA, AAA, and AFA are a small percentage of the total number of professionals. The political power that could be derived from a much higher percent of membership could be huge, and should become a goal for both the associations and their members.

Participation in professional organization can start at the undergraduate level. Preprofessional students should be encouraged to attend meetings, participate in the organization, and socialize with other professionals in order to grasp the ideals of the profession.

Self-regulation and Autonomy

In order for the business profession to reach higher levels of autonomy, it is important that all prior elements on the wheel of professionalism are met. Professionals who have been educated in the manner that is consistent with the standards of professionalism can wield political power and influence in society.[38] They will be able to negotiate the dynamics of their employment in much more effective ways.[39] This will allow them to resist managerial pressure and truly work for the benefit of all stakeholders.[40]

Conclusion

This chapter has outlined a path for business programs to build curricular changes that enhance the education and development of business professionals. These additions build on the expertise taught to business students during their college years and increase their professional identity. In the next few chapters, we use our experiences at our college to detail a curricular plan of change.

Notes

1. Khurana (2007), p. 362.
2. Nino (2011); Khurana (2007).
3. Nino (2011); Trank and Rynes (2003).
4. Trank and Rynes (2003).
5. Chitty and Black (2011).
6. Thomas and Hewitt (2011); Hall (1968); Schein and Kommers (1972).
7. Gentile (2010).

8. American Bar Association (2016).

9. Trank and Rynes (2003).

10. Cohen (1981).

11. Cohen (1981).

12. Bixler and Bixler (1959); Friedson (1994).

13. Colby, Ehrlich, Sullivan, and Dolle (2011); Miller (1985).

14. Chitty and Black (2011).

15. Adam and Miller (2001).

16. Rest and Narvaez (1994).

17. Rest and Narvaez (1994).

18. March and McCormack (2009).

19. Gregg and Stoner (2008); March and McCormack (2009).

20. Trank and Rynes (2003).

21. Colby, Ehrlich, Sullivan, and Dolle (2011).

22. Kuhn (1970).

23. Creswell (2009).

24. Chitty and Black (2011).

25. Donaldson and Preston (1995).

26. Brenner (1992).

27. Donaldson and Preston (1995).

28. Abbott (1988); Freidson (1984).

29. Hall (1968).

30. Mackey and Sisodia (2014).

31. Colby, Ehrlich, Sullivan, and Dolle (2011); Nino (2014).

32. Khurana (2007); Nino (2014).

33. Colby, Ehrlich, Sullivan, and Dolle (2011); Jacoby (2009).

34. Abbott (1988); Freidson (1984); Hall (1968).

35. Khurana and Nohria (2008).

36. Freidson (1994); Freidson (2001).

37. Freidson (2001).

38. Brint (1996); Friedson (2001).

39. Friedson (2001).

40. Kanter (2010); Khurana (2007).

PART 3

Foundation of Ethics and Repeating Themes in Business Curriculum

CHAPTER 4

Framing Ethics Using a Liberal Arts Integrated Approach

The Master said, "I cannot enlighten a mind that is not already struggling to understand or provide the words to a tongue that is not already struggling to speak. If I hold up one corner of a problem and the student does not come back with the other three, I do not repeat the lesson."

—Confucius[1]

Keywords

Business education, higher education, professionalism, foundation in ethics, ethical leadership, moral sensitivity, moral judgment, moral motivation, moral action

Introduction

As pointed out in the prior chapter, the first element on the wheel of professionalism is a foundation in ethics, thus recognizing the importance of this element in developing future professionals. Business educators have struggled with approaches to improve the ethical practices of business students. On the one hand, the business discipline is already heavy with technical knowledge that students must attain in the various subjects such as accounting, finance, marketing, management, information technology, international business, business law, economics, basic writing, public speaking, and mathematics. On the other hand, developing "professionals," as was discussed in prior chapters, is different from developing "experts." Business subjects are critical for students to become employable and valuable in the job market. Thus, faculty may believe that adding an additional requirement to the major, such as ethics, would tip the business degree to unreasonable levels. Many business schools recommend a course in ethics, but do not require it. Because most employers do not expect this knowledge, the conventional wisdom is that it is more valuable to have a business applicant be well versed in accounting, finance, and information technology than ethical philosophies. What good would that knowledge do to an employer? We attempt to answer this question below.

As we have discussed, business education has been influenced by historical and ideological events. Another strong influence on business education is the main accrediting agency for business programs in the United States, namely, the AACSB. This agency has the most authoritative power to dictate requirements at business schools. In 2003, the AACSB included a recommendation that all business school curricula include content covering ethical practices as a requirement for accreditation; however, they did not specify how business schools should incorporate this requirement into current courses and/or course sequences.[2] Instead, the AACSB allowed business programs to decide how they would integrate ethical curriculum within their courses and did not require a single course on ethics for accreditation.[3]

Thus, the teaching of professional ethics in business coursework has been inconsistent.[4] Many deans from business schools have claimed that ethics and professional training were integrated in several courses, such as marketing, finance, operations management, accounting, and strategic management. However, this fails to address the primary concern of including content specifically focused on ethical development, moral courage, and decision making. Swanson reported that a large number of business professors found it burdensome to include well-developed case points on ethics.[5] Swanson further explained that the professors rationalized their decision based on the desire to cover the required material in the courses, as well as their lack of training in teaching these concepts effectively. This deficient training influences the moral development of business students. To address this deficit, we will discuss the benefits of and approaches to ethical training that can be used. Developing professionals is a responsibility of the educational institutions and not a choice; ignoring this responsibility will only lead to more of the same, namely business students who graduate without the commitment and skills to become socially responsible business managers.

As quoted above, Confucius said that if students are not ready to struggle with the subject matter, then it is futile to offer the lesson at all. Having a foundational course in business ethics allows the students to relate to cases from different business subjects (as suggested by the AACSB) that deal with ethical issues. Without this foundation, students learn the ethical cases, only to understand that one company followed the letter of the law, and another company did not. This is inadequate in terms of educating future professionals on how to become effective and autonomous business leaders who consider the consequences of their decisions and actions on communities and society.

Foundation in Ethics

Based on our review of the literature and the need to graduate professional students who are ready to make responsible managerial decisions, we are recommending a consistent approach of adopting a foundational course in ethics in all business programs. We recommend that this course be focused a bit more on the student or the individual rather than the stakeholders' approach taken in many business ethics texts. Developing students' ethical judgment should be the goal of the course, in addition to familiarizing them with corporate governance practices as required by the AACSB. The AACSB has four broad categories of emphasis:

- responsibility of business in society,
- ethical leadership,
- ethical decision making, and
- corporate governance (AACSB).

Our approach emphasizes the second and third components, assuming that coverage for business in society and corporate governance can take place in other business courses. Below, we detail our approach for this foundational course. We believe that the elements below should be the core of a foundational course on ethics, emphasizing moral development of the individual. Taking appropriate class time on these two areas cement learning the foundation for the other courses. We also sequenced the elements as shown in Figure 4.1 below attempting to build a foundation that leads to ethical action. This underscores that the overall approach should be based on the model developed by Rest, as described below.[6]

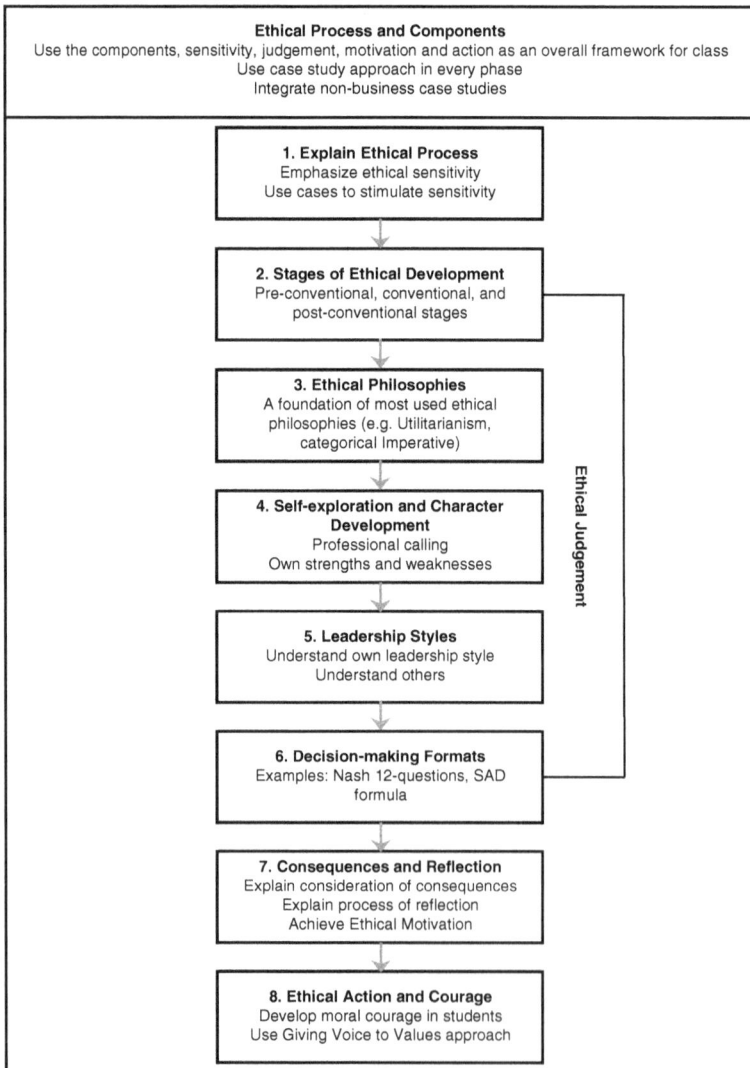

Figure 4.1 Foundational Course of Ethics—A Sequenced Model

Moral Judgment by Understanding the Components of Ethical Action

To show the process of ethical behavior, it is important to start with the components of ethical process as developed in the Rest model, and later explained by Narvaez et al. in the EthEx Series.[7] The components "moral sensitivity," "moral judgment," "moral motivation," and "moral action," if taken in sequence, provide a good path for educators to stimulate "ethical action."

Moral Sensitivity

This is the stage of recognizing that there is an ethical issue at play, as well as the feeling of conflict and uneasiness, if no action is taken. Stimulating ethical sensitivity requires taking a closer look at ethical situations, connecting and framing others' points of view, and responding to diversity while controlling social bias.

Moral Judgment

This is the reasoning process that a person goes through before deciding on an appropriate action. This involves critical and creative thinking in identifying alternatives for action. Moral judgment requires a good foundation in ethics, including judgment criteria, understanding of consequences, and reflecting on outcomes.

Moral Motivation

This is the process of sorting through personal goals, values, loyalties, and motivation. It is also the phase of integrating the moral sensitivity and judgment to build the motivation for ethical action. In this phase, a person examines their loyalties to the different groups involved in the decision. Assuming a correct process of sensitivity and judgment has occurred, an individual is reasonably motivated to take the next step.

Moral Action

This is the implementation of the ethical choice and following through with the decision despite hardship. In this stage what is required is to cultivate courage and to assert concerns respectfully. In this chapter, we focus on the "ethical judgment" element by laying a foundation of knowledge about ethics, as well as the reasoning process one goes through when they encounter an ethical issue. This develops students' ethical capacity. In the next chapter, we emphasize to educators the importance of developing students' "moral sensitivity" and "moral motivation" before expecting "moral action." Given that research shows that business students are less interested in social agency, it is pivotal that educators spend more time on teasing out the ethical components of sensitivity and motivation to develop students' professionalism.

Once students understand this framework, the course can shift to the next theoretical framework explaining the stages of ethical development (e.g., preconventional, conventional, postconventional).

Moral Judgment by Understanding Stages of Ethical Development

Another critical aspect of this unit is that students learn how character follows a developmental pattern. Human beings advance in ethical reasoning based on an increase in sophistication and experiences. Classroom coverage of Kohlberg's stages of moral development allows students to explore their own development of sophistication and cross-referencing in their reasoning, using the defined levels in the model: preconventional, conventional, and postconventional levels. Barger summarized Kohlberg's levels and stages in Table 4.1.[8]

Table 4.1 Kohlberg's Stages and Levels Summarized

Stage	Level	Social Orientation
1	Preconventional	• Responds to obedience and punishment
2	Preconventional	• Individualistic, tends to be instrumental, ability to exchange
3	Conventional	• Good boy/girl, interpersonal decorum
4	Conventional	• Follows law and order
5	Postconventional	• Social contract, obligation to society members
6	Postconventional	• Principled conscience, nonarbitrary social cooperation

Adapted from Barger (2000), Chapter 8

Following up with a few schemas from Rest's Defining Issues Test (DIT) can demonstrate to students that ethical reasoning is a journey and not a short trip, but that it is worth the cost of finding meaning as they develop their life paths.

Although Kohlberg's theory of moral development has been critiqued by many scholars, it still remains one of the most relevant platforms for ethical development. Most of the criticisms of Kohlberg's theory have centered around the validity of testing of subjects, as well as the use of "reasoning" as the strongest component of judging ethical development. Many scholars suggested using ethical behavior as the benchmark. Critics have questioned whether the capacity for reasoning, as suggested by Kohlberg, will consistently lead to ethical action.[9] Although some scholars questioned Kohlberg's hard stages of ethical development, there is supporting evidence to his assumption of a progression of moral development with age through a sequenced set of stages[10].

For the most part, students are excited about learning the moral schemas and moral levels. Suddenly they begin to analyze situations and actors around them, framing them in a different light and cross-referencing behavior against the moral levels in ethical development.[11] Understanding degrees of sophistication (e.g., preconventional, conventional, postconventional) in decision making opens up a student's view of life situations. They become more aware of people's behavior, including friends, family members, business colleagues, decision makers, and educators. The experience in judging ethical situations helps build self-concept and autonomy, leading to advancement in their professional thinking.

Foundation in Ethical Philosophies

In his recent text on Organizational Ethics, Johnson devotes a full section to teaching the most relevant ethical philosophies.[12] He argues that "ethical theories are critical to personal and collective ethical practice." These foundational theories are meant to show a student (especially a preprofessional) how to identify and define a problem, think systematically, view the issue from many different perspectives, and understand guidelines for decision making. All these skills are needed for appropriate ethical judgment, as noted by the Rest model.[13] Asking students to judge on the facts of the case, without having a foundation in ethics, can lead students to make judgments based on the prescribed law in the situation. Using only the prescribed law often leads students to think at preconventional levels, which according to Kohlberg, results in conformity and mimicking others' actions as the common standard.[14] Rather, this comprehensive approach of starting with an ethical foundation allows students to differentiate between ethics and the law.

There are many ethical-philosophies that can be studied by students in such a course. The following are the most common frameworks that students should understand prior to approaching ethical situations. It is important for the educator to emphasize that these are theoretical frameworks for understanding situations rather than a prescription to address ethical ailments. Together they help students understand that multiple approaches can be used in ethical decision making.

- Utilitarianism: Do the greatest good for the greatest number of people evaluation. This is a helpful framework for students to understand, since many business conflicts are resolved based on this model. Once understood, students often refer to this framework to explain business case studies, or business situations they come across in their internships or daily life.
- Kant's Categorical Imperative: Do what is right despite the consequences of evaluation. Students relate to this one based on personal or family experiences they have experienced. It is important that students understand that this framework represents a postconventional approach in the Kohlberg model. This allows them to elevate their thinking to seek higher ethical standards when judging situations.
- Rawl's Justice as Fairness: Balance freedom and equality evaluation. This is beneficial for students to understand the advantages of societal equality, compensatory benefits, and the use of a nondiscriminatory process. Using this philosophy, students learn empathy and ethical sensitivity that are beyond the logical business flow they are used to when solving a business case.

- Aristotelian Ethics: Live well and do good evaluation. Using this philosophy, students search for their own higher purpose, which allows them to live well and achieve their potential while they are contributing positively to society.
- Confucianism: Build healthy relationships evaluation. Students learn that to build a better society, they have to foster loving and benevolent relationships with their families, friends, and their external communities.
- Altruism: Build concern for others: The ethics of care evaluation. Students' awareness of this normative, and often feminist, philosophy allows them to respond differently to situations based on the circumstances and individuals involved, using a customized and caring approach. This is a contrasting philosophy to the earlier ones that emphasize the use of universal rules.

The intent of this chapter is to examine how business students can use these theories, and explain the many decisions made throughout history. They are great models for an educator to use with any case study and point to how a person, an organization, or a company may have arrived at the decision that they did. Having these different models allow students to reflect back on situations, try different models, and see which one best fits the scenario. Teaching ethics without teaching the different frameworks places the student in a maze without direction. Thus, a foundational course is necessary for students to engage in ethical decision making. This is also an opportune time to explain "theory and theoretical frameworks" to business students, since this topic is also important in developing professionals.

Moreover, these philosophies show students the reality of using more than one approach to a situation. Yet, often, after students learn the different philosophies, they feel a bit lost, given that any of these frameworks might justify the decision made. It is then that the educator needs to step in and help students understand why a selected framework may be more appropriate for the situation at hand. Many ethics courses do not do this. They may cover the different philosophies, but the priority or the fit of one framework over the other is not examined. This can lead students to think that as long as they pick their favorite philosophy, they must be on the correct path in solving an ethical dilemma. Therefore, educators should point out that the philosophies are theoretical frameworks to think about a situation, but certainly not the solution to it. Below, we discuss the components of ethical action and we define this model as the appropriate approach to guide students to sound decisions.[15]

One may argue that a business class is not the place to learn these philosophies and this is partly true, since these frameworks could be covered in a philosophy class. The problem is that when business students learn this in a philosophy class, they classify this knowledge as "general education" or material that is unnecessary for their professional development. They also frequently fail to see the connection between this knowledge and their future careers. Many of our students, who have taken a course on ethics, prior to taking a business ethics course, claim that they only made sense of the philosophies, and their application, in the business curriculum. This could be related to the repetition of learning this knowledge, but it may also reflect having to apply the material in a business context.

Self-exploration and Character Development

Another reason for offering a single course in the second or third year of a business student undergraduate program is the course's connection to concepts of professionalism. Specifically, this course lends itself well to helping students strengthen self-concept, autonomy, and social agency. Students can begin the course by doing a realistic self-appraisal of their own professionalism, using the questionnaire listed in Table 2.2, as mentioned before.

From Johnson's text *Organizational Ethics*, students use the section on self-appraisal, discovering vocation and calling, identifying personal values, developing character, creating a moral identity, and drawing on spiritual resources.[16] Students take the journey to identify their personal gifts and interest and then map the results to educational and professional goals. One part of this module is on character development. Students begin to understand the difference between personal characteristics (e.g., strengths and weaknesses) and virtues. They discover the path to develop their own virtues and the rewards of having them. Students also learn about a positive path of character development and the reasons they should aspire to in-depth self-exploration and self-actualization.

This module can be covered in a few weeks and students really enjoy this personal development opportunity, as they find it meaningful and inspiring. Many students report that when selecting business as a major, they had not done a lot of thinking about their own personal gifts or their calling. Thus, having this opportunity of self-exploration encourages deeper thinking about their future profession and its connection to their self-development path.

Ethical Leadership and Different Styles

Leadership is another element that is important in developing professionals' self-concept, and we devote an entire chapter later, attempting to integrate the subject into business education. But in business ethics, it is important to engage students in learning about the challenges of ethical leadership. Having completed some self-exploration, students are ready to look outside of themselves. Although this is not a course on leadership, ethical leadership is what we are seeking in future business managers. Thus, analyses of leadership styles helps prepare students for future business positions where they will be either leading and managing or being lead and managed. Therefore, an introduction of the different styles of good and bad leadership allows students to examine both historical and contemporary leaders. It is helpful to teach students the different styles of leadership, and sources such as Jean Lipman-Blumen and Barbara Kellerman have extensive discussions of good and bad styles.[17] Additionally, students should explore normative leadership theories such as transformational, servant, authentic, and responsible leadership, attempting to discover their own natural styles. We consider this component as optional but helpful in an ethics class.

Moral Judgment by Understanding Decision-making Formats

Once students become familiar with the ethical philosophies, leadership styles, and the components of ethical behavior, they are in need of methodological tools that can help them make decisions. This assumes that students have framed the situation and its actors in a theoretical framework, such as Kidder's ethical checkpoints, the SAD formula, and Nash's 12 questions. These tools can be characterized as flowcharts, which can help students make better choices as they navigate through normal everyday conflicts in the work environment. Most of these tools require students to recognize the situation, gather details and analyze, and make the decision. Following is a quick schematic of Kidder's Ethical Checkpoints[18]:

1. Checkpoint: Recognize that there is a moral issue
2. Checkpoint: Determine the actors in the situation
3. Checkpoint: Gather the relevant facts
4. Checkpoint: Test for right-versus-wrong issues, in order to evaluate correct and incorrect approaches to handle the situation
5. Checkpoint: Test for right-versus-right paradigms to understand the various possible alternatives available, while examining loyalties to self, communities, and overall society
6. Checkpoint: Apply ethical standards and perspectives
7. Checkpoint: Look for a third way to reconcile and create win–win solutions
8. Checkpoint: Make the decision
9. Checkpoint: Revisit and reflect on the decision

These formats allow students to use a step-by-step approach to ensure a carefully thought-out decision, thus avoiding ethical blunders. If students are able to learn a process to evaluate ethical dilemmas, they are much more likely to work through such situations more effectively.

Ethical Motivation: Develop Students' Ability to Evaluate Consequences

Connecting decisions to their consequences is an important and difficult skill, even for experienced professionals. This skill requires thinking and anticipating short- and long-term consequences and considering all the individuals and stakeholders who may be affected by an action. The best approach to develop this skill with students is through case studies. Case studies permit students to review the case with hindsight ability. In the next chapter, we discuss the Bernie Madoff case, which has a focus on evaluating the consequences.

Reflection is a meta-cognitive skill involving the process of thinking about thinking or having the intention to set-aside time for thinking.[19] Reflection is the process of thinking about one's decision process and outcomes. In the Nixon case study (below), we use discussion questions that prompt students to reflect. We suggest that educators create opportunities that allow for reflection. Also, responding to case studies in writing encourages students to reflect. This phase highlights the essence of developing ethical motivation as referred to in the Rest Model.

Ethical Action and Courage

It is important that students understand the courage needed for ethical action. Mary Gentile in her book *Giving Voice to Values* lays an excellent foundation for working individuals to develop a plan of action, once a decision to act has been made. Educators can benefit from adopting her approach when teaching this section. Furthermore, educators need to remind students that ethical action takes hard work and perseverance but it does have rewards.

Sequenced Approach

In summary, we believe a foundational course in ethics should focus on the individual; in this case, the students. Additionally, the course should build a foundation in sequence based on student-readiness for the information. For example, students are not ready to learn about ethical philosophies until they have understood the Rest model and how the components of sensitivity, judgment, motivation, and action build on each other. In addition, students should only be taught ethical action and courage, after understanding sound ethical judgment, as well as reflection and evaluation of consequences. Finally, the course should include all the following components, in order for students to achieve improved ethical judgment skills:

1. Moral judgment by understanding the components of ethical action as explained above. The ethical components should be the compass for the faculty during the course, as students develop in their moral judgment. After explaining the model to students, educators should emphasize ethical sensitivity and tease out using one to two case studies.

2. Understanding stages of ethical development, in order to distinguish between low levels of ethical judgment at the preconventional levels and high levels of ethical judgment at the postconventional stages.
3. Understanding of ethical philosophies and their application in order to enhance ethical judgment.
4. Self-exploration and character development, in order for the course to have a student-focused approach.
5. Understanding different leadership styles in order to assess future work environment and its players.
6. Develop students' ability to focus on consequences and to reflect in order to reach ethical motivation stage.
7. Moral judgment by understanding decision-making formats.
8. Ethical action and courage.

Above is a graph summarizing our approach to teaching a foundational course on ethics (Figure 4.1). This graph sequences the theoretical material as we envision it to be taught in the classroom. We find this as an effective approach to learn the concepts and apply them to cases. Keep in mind, we stress that educators should use the case-study approach to have students think and experience every phase. We also encourage the use of nonbusiness cases as we discuss below.

Integrating Examples from Disciplines Other than Business

A course in business ethics also provides the opportunity for faculty to use case studies that are not taken from business. Given that this course is meant to be a foundational one on business ethics, it may be best to draw cases from other disciplines such as history and political science (and this can also reintroduce important events). We urge educators to reduce the use of business or leadership cases that may bias students against the business world. Students can apply their analytical skills to business situations in the future. Additionally, using examples from other fields allows students to view ethical conflicts objectively without infusing their own business biases onto the situation.

An example of a successful case that we used in this course is about Richard Nixon as a leader. The case study, readings, and questions were developed by Professor of History, Dr. Laura McEnaney, in collaboration with assigned readings on leadership. While the readings show different "sides" of Nixon, the focus of the case is on the lack of ethical reasoning and judgment. Scenes from the film Frost/Nixon were used to highlight President Nixon's leadership style and ethical reasoning. Toward the end, one scene shows his deep regret for the decisions he made during Watergate. Yet, his deepest regret is how he may have influenced young people's views about the political process. This invites students to engage in deep reflection and long-term thinking. From the readings, they see that President Nixon abused his power by trying to control all the actors and events around him. Rather than think of the consequences of his actions, he only thought of power and control. While he may have been a strong leader, who was credited with many good decisions and changes during the presidency, he still was unable to weigh the consequences of having his schemes discovered and the influence of that on the American people and the country. Below is our approach to presenting the case study and for the discussion with students:

Case Study Readings: President Richard Nixon and His leadership

In addition to a Brief Timeline of Events for Watergate (from the Washington Post[a]), students read:

- Kellerman, B. (2004). Bad leadership: What it is, how it happens, why it matters. Harvard Business Press, Chapters 1–3
- Patterson, J. T. (1996). Grand Expectations: The United States, 1945–1974. Oxford University Press, 771–782

Students are asked to reflect on the following questions:

- Richard Nixon was a leader of both a nation and a political party. What does this handling of Watergate suggest about the leadership *in partisan politics?*

---

[a]The Timeline of Events can be obtained online using the following link: http://watergate.info/chronology/brief-timeline-of-events

- How would you characterize Nixon's leadership style using some of the types listed in Kellerman: incompetent, rigid, corrupt, or insular?
- Kellerman analyzes the role of followers when leaders go astray. What is your assessment of the why some of "the president's men" engineered the break-in and participated in the cover-up? How do you assess their responsibility in this scandal? Did they have alternatives?
- Historian Stanley Kutler argues that Richard Nixon destroyed the presidency to save the president. Do you agree with this analysis of Nixon's leadership?
- President Ford, Nixon's successor, said in 1984 that Nixon owed the nation an apology. Should leaders apologize after such scandal? Would that have helped in any way? What is the function of an apology in modern politics?
- What does Watergate suggest to you about the perils and possibilities of leadership? What are the cautionary tales in this episode for your generation—as either leaders or followers?
- Richard Nixon is the most famous graduate of Whittier College. How can or should Whittier use the history of Nixon to teach leadership? Should we lean into what his presidency can teach us, or should we keep a healthy distance from this history? Could you advise Whittier College's President about how to use Nixon's legacy for our school?

Additional Questions by Co-instructor:
- Using the Kohlberg model, what stage of moral development was President Nixon utilizing during Watergate? How would you help President Nixon advance his ethical reasoning during the Watergate Scandal?
- Using Rest's model of ethical behavior (i.e., ethical sensitivity, ethical judgment, ethical motivation, ethical action), which component did Nixon fail to exercise?[20]
- In hindsight, had President Nixon thought of the consequences or had followers who had the courage to warn him of the consequences, would he have acted in the same manner? Why or why not?

Other cases and modules:

While there are many excellent nonbusiness leadership cases and modules that can be used in a foundational business ethics class, we mention a few below that have been used successfully in coordination with Professor John Bak, who teaches documentary film:

- Robert McNamara, American business executive and the eighth Secretary of Defense, serving from 1961 to 1968 under Presidents John F. Kennedy and Lyndon B. Johnson. This case can be used along with the documentary *Fog of War*, where Robert McNamara reflects on 11 lessons he learned through his career, most notably on decisions made that resolved the Cuban missile crisis and prolonged the Vietnam War.
- Leadership analysis of Adolph Hitler. This case can be used with filmmaker Leni Riefenstahl's *Triumph of the Will* documentary that shows Hitler consolidating power in 1934, and gaining a tremendous followership in Germany prior to and during the Holocaust. In this leadership analysis, students struggle to see Hitler as a widely followed leader who appealed to the nationalistic feelings of his followers. Once he was elected, he created institutions to support his power, and eventually used fear-of-the-other, threats, and execution/murder to maintain his power, especially during the Holocaust. Students learn how leadership can change over time and become not just toxic but evil. Ethical leadership analysis can include lessons on balance of power, toxic leadership, and the ability to discern when leaders move from healthy, strong leadership to toxic leadership.

Link to Professionalism and Readiness for the AACSB Integrated Model

Developing an ethical approach to business situations can be a daunting task. The AACSB selected an integrated approach to ethics education, in order for students to see ethical principles applied in various business subjects such as marketing, finance, accounting, and international business.

This approach is also a valuable approach since students would be exposed to enough repetition of the concepts to memorize and internalize them. However, the AACSB method is deficient, since it does not take into account that students have not learned the principles to be able to apply them. Students need to advance in moral development prior to being exposed to the integration described by the AACSB. Building a foundation using the process of ethical judgment with all the other steps suggested above, and then using the AACSB integrated model in all business courses helps students internalize the foundation.[21] Then, repeating the process they have learned in different sub-disciplines, such as marketing, accounting, finance, and management, allows for reexamination of concepts and reflections. In the next chapter, we show how educators can use the "repeat process" to integrate ethics in all business offerings, after students have completed a foundational course.

Notes

1. Legge (2009).
2. Miles, Hazeldine, and Munilla (2004).
3. Miles, Hazeldine, and Munilla (2004); Swanson and Frederick (2003).
4. Miles, Hazeldine, and Munilla (2004); Swanson and Frederick (2001).
5. Swanson (2004).
6. Rest (1984).
7. Rest (1984); Narvaez and Endicott (2009c); Navaraez and Lies (2009a); Navaraez (2009b)
8. Barger (2000).
9. Rest, Bebeau, Thoma, and Bebeau (1999).
10. Kohlberg (1976).
11. Rest (1984, 1986).
12. Johnson (2016).
13. Rest (1984, 1986).
14. Kohlberg (1973).
15. Rest (1984, 1986).
16. Johnson (2016).

17. Lipman-Blumen (2000); Kellerman (2004).
18. Johnson (2013), Chapter 7
19. Narvaez and Bock (2009).
20. Rest (1984).
21. Rest (1984).

CHAPTER 5

Building Ethical Sensitivity Before Ethical Action

"Before you act, listen.

Before you react, think.

Before you spend, earn.

Before you criticize, wait.

Before you pray, forgive.

Before you quit, try."

—Ernst Hemingway[1]

Keywords

Business education, higher education, professionalism, foundation in ethics, ethical leadership, ethical sensitivity, ethical judgment, ethical motivation, ethical action, Fink's taxonomy of significant learning

Introduction

Calls for developing reflective skills by business students have been made by many scholars.[2] Most definitions or descriptions of professionalism have an underlying message, namely that the very nature of professional work requires the ability to be able to place themselves in the "shoes" of the other. Often this requires one to imagine oneself in the position of the other and to see situations through their eyes. The manner by which educators can accomplish this is often elusive and challenging, especially when economic pressures and academic capitalism may work against the reflection that is needed. Where Durkheim and Larson considered the rise of a professional class to be a necessary response to industrialization, others, a century later, are beginning to call on professionalism in response to corporate and governmental powers.[3] Whatever the motivation, many agree that developing professionals has become an increasingly urgent task. Our view is that business educators need to situate the important concept of professionalism at the core of the mission for business education. To do so, educators need to better understand the critical importance of developing autonomous, reflective professionals. Business professionals are the captains of industry in society and their decisions influence every organization, every home, and every person. The 2008 financial crisis bears witness to this. But the danger to society does not always occur due to economic cycles and political pressures. As Brint stated, it is in the rise of the "expert" class and mass population of technicians, who fail to consider the influence of their decisions on society.[4] In contrast, sociologists have always envisioned a class of reflective, autonomous professionals to be a powerful strata working to balance and negotiate corporate and government interest and society.

In the last chapter, we discussed the importance of teaching the fundamentals of ethics using a foundational course on ethics. In this chapter, we explore the AACSB approach of integrating ethics in every sub-discipline in the business curriculum, and suggest an approach to make this process more effective. We agree with the AACSB approach that weaving of ethics into the business subject, such as marketing, accounting, and finance, allows for repetition and comprehension. We also believe that this approach, implemented as suggested in this chapter, improves students' ability to arrive at ethical decisions and actions more frequently.

The current approach to ethics in the business curriculum is often presented in the form of case studies or ethical scenarios, along with a description of the current laws applying to the specific discipline. This is a good approach, but may lack the deeper discussion about the precursors to and elements of ethical behavior in the cases/scenarios. The work of Rest is crucial in understanding that ethical action has its roots in ethical sensitivity, ethical judgment, and ethical motivation.[5] The previous chapter described the process of developing ethical judgment; this chapter will focus on the other three elements. The emphasis on ethical sensitivity and motivation should, in most cases, prepare students to engage in ethical action, which we will show through examples in this chapter. Because these steps, as well as Rest's comprehensive approach are so important, we strongly recommend that business educators become familiar with the ideas below, as steps in developing students' professionalism.

Using the Ethical Model in the Classroom

Narvaez and Endicott, Narvaez and Bock, Narvaez and Lies wrote four books—the EthEx Series—detailing the four main psychological processes involved in behaving ethically.[6] We use their books to help explain these elements as shown in Figure 5.1. They suggest that their material is not a curriculum that is taught in a separate class, but a method all educators can adopt in their courses. This is consistent with the AACSB approach of weaving ethics in the curriculum of business education.

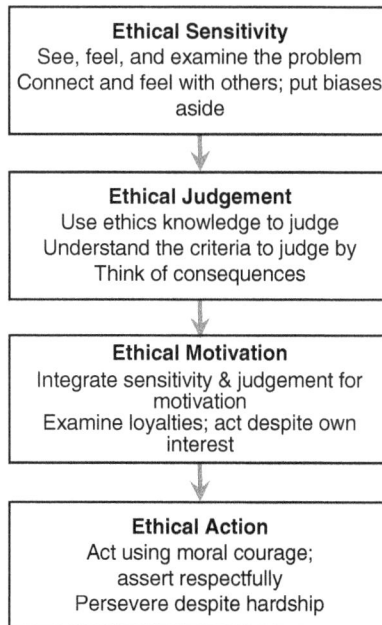

Ethical Sensitivity
See, feel, and examine the problem
Connect and feel with others; put biases aside

↓

Ethical Judgement
Use ethics knowledge to judge
Understand the criteria to judge by
Think of consequences

↓

Ethical Motivation
Integrate sensitivity & judgement for motivation
Examine loyalties; act despite own interest

↓

Ethical Action
Act using moral courage;
assert respectfully
Persevere despite hardship

Figure 5.1 Ethical Process Model

In their introduction, they use an example to describe the process of ethical action. We have adapted their process, using our own examples.

Short Vignette

Imagine a sales and marketing executive who is working on a multi-million dollar product sale to a key customer. The executive is aware of several product deficiencies. He has not mentioned them to the customer, in fear of losing the sale. It is quarter-end and the executive is trying to meet his financial goals that are tied to other teams' goals and other executives as well. What should the executive do?

It is essential that the executive knows what ethical behavior is, which in this case is to disclose product deficiencies to the customer. It is always helpful to visualize ethical failure, prior to thinking about ethical behavior. For example, think of the possibility of the customer learning about the deficiencies from other sources. The result would no doubt be to lose the customer permanently. To get to this point likely means that there were ethical misjudgments along the way. First, the executive may recognize the dissatisfaction from the customer or the customer could be asking several questions around the deficiencies. The executive may have felt the need to disclose the problems before, but decided not to several times. He may have been concerned and spent hours in the night worrying about the non-disclosure. He may have gone through an analysis of what actions might be taken and what outcomes might occur. But, then the executive must reason through the choices and decide on the possible actions. Next, the executive would prioritize the chosen ethical action over other needs and motives. For example, the executive may need to let his team down and give up his anticipated bonus. Then he would need to persevere until the action is completed, which may mean conflicts with his boss or team members. It is obvious that there are many places, where ethical misjudgment may occur.

In order for the right ethical process to occur, one needs to understand the components of ethical action well. We start by dissecting ethical sensitivity and ethical motivation, in order to understand these elements further. In the previous chapter, we covered "ethical judgment." All three elements should occur prior to ethical action. We feel that in order to follow the AACSB approach of integrating ethics in all courses, business faculty need to be fully versed in these components, and how to weave them into the case studies incorporated in their disciplines.

Ethical Sensitivity

Ethical sensitivity is the recognition of an ethical problem or dilemma. It is the ability to notice cues of a moral situation at hand and feel conflict because of it. To be ethically sensitive, one needs to interpret the situation and then: feel compelled to act; determine who is involved; what actions must be taken; and what possible reaction and outcomes might occur. Following is an outline of necessary skills to become proficient at this task:[7]

ES-1: Reading and Expressing Emotion

This is a very important skill for business students and one that is often ignored in the teaching of ethical action. This skill requires the ability to feel and read surrounding emotions of others, when a situation happens. It also requires the identification with the needs and feelings of self and others.

ES-2: Taking the Perspectives of Others

This task requires extensive practice and experience. Once presenting students with a case, an educator needs to walk students through the process of taking others' perspectives in the situation. Students need to practice taking the perspective of someone in their own culture as well as someone outside of their culture. This builds empathy, tolerance, as well as motivation to execute ethical action.

ES-3: Connecting to Others

This skill involves expanding one's sense of concern to include others, both locally and globally. This connection to others compels one to think of their own actions in terms of its effect on a broader group beyond the self. This sense of connection encourages a person to show care and concern for others. Students need to learn how to connect positively to others, show friendship, and feel the rewards of this behavior.

ES-4: Responding to Diversity

There is a significant effort in higher education to expose students to diverse cultures and groups. This cultural awareness can also help to develop students' ethical sensitivity. When students work with different groups, they learn and understand how cultural differences can lead to conflicts and misunderstandings. This develops students' appreciation and skills in dealing with such conflicts. It also helps them shift using one culture code to another to resolve misunderstandings. While culture is often applied to large entities, educators need to help students think of culture in a narrow sense, such as "school culture," "business culture," or "college culture."

ES-5: Controlling Social Bias

This is another skill that faculty need to practice with students while discussing appropriate case studies. Social bias is part of human nature and people are more comfortable with familiar groups, similar ways of thinking, and similar social groups. To counter one's social bias is a skill that requires effort, awareness, and mindful processes that when applied recognize and control prejudice. This skill stimulates the rethinking of personal habits, shaping one's judgments and actions into more respectful ways of interacting in society.

ES-6: Interpreting Situations

This involves developing the creative skills to generate multiple interpretations of a situation to reach deeper understanding of it. It also allows for developing multiple alternatives to solve a problem at hand, thus avoiding the pitfalls of inter-social interpretation. Being able to generate different ways to solve a problem helps individuals avoid the repeat of their mistakes. This element facilitates the reexamination of an issue from different angles, generating both interpretation of perspectives and possible solutions.

ES-7: Communicating Well

These skills will not be effective without the enhancement of written, spoken, listening, and nonverbal communication. Faculty can emphasize the development of these skills as they guide students in solving, discussing, and writing out solutions to case studies. It is also important for faculty to stress the social context of communication and where and how different types of communication (e.g., one-on-one, small group, large group, etc.) are more appropriate than others.

Following is a case study that we borrow from Johnson's text *Organizational Ethics* to illustrate how to guide students through the process of practicing ethical sensitivity.

This is a terrific case to discuss how ethical sensitivity is important to reach some conclusions on the case. Without using the platform of ethical sensitivity, students may resort only to judge based on the local laws in region or state, but using all the components above, students start to appreciate how culture plays a role in the laws in different places in the world. It is also worthwhile to explain to the students that ethical sensitivity is about one's ability to examine and reexamine an issue from multiple angles, get closer to the problem and not disregard it, feel it as if you were in the situation, and then judge with an ethical eye.

Case Study 13.1

The Right to be Forgotten[8]

Individual privacy is a fundamental right in both the United States and Europe. However, the two regions define this right very differently. In the United States, privacy is "the right to be left alone" and free press and free speech rights often supersede this right. This view of privacy was illustrated by a California Supreme Court ruling that journalists could publicize the sexual orientation of a gay man who stopped an assassination attempt on former President Gerald Ford. The hero repeatedly asked the press not to reveal this information, which was hidden from his family, but the court ruled that helping to protect the president had made him a public figure. In Europe, dignity underlies privacy concerns. According to Zurich law professor Rolf Weber, Europeans consider "dignity, honor and the right to private life: the most fundamental rights." There is the "right for the [moral and legal] integrity of a person not to be infringed and for a sphere of privacy to be maintained and distinguished."[a] The European Court of Human Rights ruled, for example, that German papers had violated Princess Caroline of Monaco's privacy rights by publishing photographs of her and her family. The tribunal noted that the pictures were taken in "a climate of continual harassment" and involved "a very strong sense of intrusion into their private life."[b]

The European Court of Justice applied the European conception of privacy to the Internet when it ruled that its citizens have the "right to be forgotten." A Spaniard petitioned the court to force Google to remove information about the auction sale of his repossessed home. He argued that this reference was irrelevant because the matter had been resolved years earlier. He asked Google to remove the pages and to ensure that news of the auction no longer appeared in search results. The Court of Justice agreed, declaring that individuals have a limited right to ask search engines to remove links with personal information if the information is "inaccurate, inadequate, irrelevant or excessive."[c] This judgment applies to all current or future Internet providers operating in Europe.

In response to the ruling, Google, which handles an estimated 85 percent of Europe's web traffic, set up a system to handle data removal requests. Applicants fill out an online form that is submitted to a team within Google's legal department, which weighs the request against the public interest. If the request is approved, the search engine then removes the web link within the 28 nations of the European Union as well as in Iceland, Norway, Switzerland, and Liechtenstein (The link would still be visible outside the region). Country data-protection regulators will decide in cases where individuals dispute Google's decision. Initially 70,000 requests came in to remove personal information. Several links to stories in *The Guardian* newspaper, including articles about a disgraced soccer referee and the ouster of former Merrill Lynch

---

[a] Learning from Europe's 'right to be forgotten' (2013).

[b] Learning from Europe's 'right to be forgotten' (2013).

[c] Factsheet on the 'Right to be Forgotten' ruling. (2014, May 13). *European Commission*. Additional sources for this section are Google restores links to some news articles after outcry (2014); Scott (June 18, 2014; July 5, 2014); Spanier (2014).

CEO Stanley O'Neill, were among the first to be removed. Google later restored several of these links after free speech advocates and journalists complained. However, opponents of the right to be forgotten worry that prominent people and corporations will use the system to delete unfavorable information about them.

The European Parliament is expected to pass digital privacy legislation that would expand the right to be forgotten to social media providers like Facebook as well as to e-commerce sites. Some U.S. observers argue that American citizens should have the same right to maintain their electronic dignity as Europeans. They then could petition Google, Bing, Yahoo, and other providers to take down embarrassing personal photos, criminal convictions and mug shots, old bankruptcy filings, caustic blog posts, and other items they would like to leave in their pasts.

Discussion Probes

1. What does the right to privacy mean to you? The right to be left alone or the right to maintain your dignity?
2. What should take precedence—the right of privacy or the right of free speech?
3. What do you think constitutes "inaccurate, inadequate, irrelevant, or excessive" information on the Internet? Can you think of any examples?
4. Should American citizens "have the right to be forgotten"?
5. What information should never be deleted from the Internet?

Recommended Approach

We recommend the use of small groups for discussion first to make students comfortable in sharing. Afterwards, educators can ask students to share best responses with the entire class.

1. Give examples of the individuals or groups who are being harmed because of privacy laws in their region? Explore the rights of these

individuals or groups. Ask students to share their own privacy stories on social media or other.

Learning point: Students may then identify with the gay man who saved President Gerald Ford's life, the individual who lost his house in foreclosure, Princess Caroline of Monaco and her family, and others from the case. It is important that the educator explores why are these people being harmed and how students identify with their needs of privacy. Students at this point may recount their own privacy violation stories from social media or other contexts and explain how they experienced and identified with individuals in the case study. Remember ethical sensitivity starts by the empathic interpretation of a situation. Ask students to weigh in on privacy needs relative to the importance of free speech.

2. Ask students to compare privacy laws in Europe and the U.S., and then ask them to discuss the merits of the laws in each country.

Learning point: In this step, students learn to appreciate diversity of cultures and what it means to live in one country versus another. Respecting U.S. laws meant that a gay man had to publicly declare his sexual identity. Living in Europe meant that the public might not find out about the ouster of Merrill Lynch CEO. Have students identify the pros and cons of the two approaches to privacy. Given that privacy laws are a "work in progress" in many countries, students are more likely to feel like engaged citizens whose participation in the political process can help benefit their lives and the lives of others.

3. Have students think about the individuals in the case such as the gay man, the Princess of Monaco, or the Spaniard with the foreclosed home. Ask students whether the contextual details of these individuals matter?

Learning point: This discussion helps students discuss social biases, and how to factor them. Also, what it means to forget to factor social biases in their ethical judgment. Students appreciate the need for the gay man to have his privacy, as well as the Princess of Monaco's right to live a normal life away from the public eye. Students also may discuss how the Spaniard may be living in a community where it is a shame to lose one's home. Considering these peculiarities expands students' thinking beyond their own social bubble.

4. Also, ask the students to discuss the questions that are already included in the case since they are helpful in going through the ethical process with its four components.

5. Have students write a two-page summary responding to the question in the case, "should American citizens have the right to be forgotten?" *Learning point*: Students do their most reflective thinking when writing papers. They also learn to communicate their thoughts as they are organizing, collecting their deepest frames of thinking and summarizing. This is an important exercise to help students think about the issues, summarize, and communicate.

This type of case encourages students to reflect on the contextual facts in the case. This expands students' judgment and their reasoning ability. Students learn to develop different interpretations of the same problem and problem-solve in multiple ways. This case is perfectly suited for a marketing or management class, but regardless of the discipline, the business educator has to learn the approach to expose the key points and stimulate the needed discussion.

Ethical Judgment

Ethical judgment is the ability to reason through problems, understand them, use different judgment criteria to evaluate them, understand the consequences of one's actions related to the problem, and reflect and cope through the process. In the previous chapter, we detailed the elements that advance students' capacities for ethical judgment. This entailed learning the foundation of ethics including using decision-making formats.

Ethical Motivation

Ethical motivation refers to the personal decision one makes to prioritize ethical action over personal motivations, loyalties, and goals. To do so requires both ethical sensitivity and ethical judgment, so one must have developed these skills in order to develop ethical motivation. This is the main reason that we emphasize building ethical sensitivity in the classroom and through social agency in community activities, which will be discussed in a later chapter.

EM-1: Respecting Others

Respecting others and their views is a sign of civility and a core societal value. Educators using examples and case studies can show that others have rights and responsibilities toward us as we do them. Also, educators must show students how respecting differences is an important value that builds tolerance and appreciation of others and otherness.

EM-2: Cultivating Conscience

To cultivate one's conscience is the ability to have self-command and patience in difficult situations, especially when one recognizes his or her ability to inflict harm on others. Managing one's ability to control impulses and manage power is an important skill in cultivating conscience. Educators can have students list things they have power over and whether they have the cultivated conscience not to abuse them.

EM-3: Acting Responsibly

This is one's desire to uphold his or her responsibilities in meeting obligations. It is also being a good steward of one's talents and assets, and acting as a responsible global citizen. Educators can provide many examples of responsible citizenship or corporate duty to society.

EM-4: Being a Community Member

Ethical motivation is fostered by active membership in the community. One must recognize and act on the opportunities to help in their societal circle or community. This requires skills of cooperation and thoughtfulness while being a part of a group.

EM-5: Finding Meaning in Life

Educators, through case studies and examples, can show students the rewards of commitment, dedication, and active citizenship. Finding meaning in life can be cultivated by focusing attention and energies around commitments that shape students' worthy goals. This is an important element whereby educators can help students define their long-term goals, as well as their higher purpose in life. Using a writing exercise, as was explained in the prior chapter, can support this. Another sub-element of this component is to help students appreciate beauty in life beyond materialistic possessions.

EM-6: Valuing Traditions and Institutions

In order to cultivate ethical motivations, educators must help students appreciate traditions and institutions in their society. If students have positive feelings toward the laws, practices, and organizations of society, they are more likely to participate in community decision making. Active citizenship leads to motivation to help others and participate in a democratic society.

EM-7: Developing Ethical Identity and Integrity

This is the goal of ethical motivation, which is to develop an ethical identity of oneself as an ethical agent. It also enables students to identify with ethical role models in order to create positive ethical identity. Ethical identity leads to ethical action since one's acts reinforce his or her self-concept.

Following is a case study that we borrow from Johnson's text *Meeting the Ethical Challenges of Leadership* to illustrate how to guide students through the process of practicing ethical motivation.

Case Study 2.1

Bernie Madoff and the Biggest Swindle in History[9], Also Show the Documentary: Frontline: The Madoff Affair[10]

For decades, Bernard (Bernie) Madoff was one of the most respected figures on Wall Street. He chaired the NASDAQ electronic trading system and the National Association of Securities Dealers, the regulatory body assigned to prevent investment fraud. He conducted business from a multistory office building in Manhattan and owned a penthouse in New York, a mansion in Florida, and a villa in France. Madoff ran an investment fund that consistently reported steady, high returns (10 percent to 12 percent) even during recessions. Potential clients eagerly sought the privilege of investing with him. All that changed, however, in December 2008, when Madoff confessed to running a pyramid or Ponzi scheme. Instead of making legitimate investments, Bernie used contributions from new victims to pay back old victims, underwrite losses in his legitimate brokerage business, and finance his lavish lifestyle. The financier cheated victims out of $65 billion, which likely makes this the largest swindle in history. While billions were funneled into his fund through U.S. and European banks and hedge funds, a number of Madoff's friends and associates were also caught in the scam, along with many charities that trusted him with their money. Even Carl Shapiro, a close friend of Madoff who loaned him $250,000 to start his business, lost $1.7 million in the scheme.

The disgraced con artist pled guilty to a number of criminal charges. In his statement to the court, he said he was "deeply sorry and ashamed" for his acts.[a] Judge Denny Chin then sentenced Madoff to 150 years in prison, well in excess of what the parole board had recommended. He called Madoff's scam "extraordinarily evil" after hearing victims describe how Bernie had destroyed their lives by stealing their life savings. He noted that the sentence was largely symbolic because Madoff (age 71 at the time of his sentencing) would die after only finishing a portion of his sentence. However, Chin argued that such symbolism was important because it would only serve as a form of retribution and deterrence, but the sentence itself would provide some measure of justice for victims.

It will take years for law enforcement officials, regulators, lawyers, victims, and others to sort through the wreckage Madoff left behind. To begin with, there are questions about how the fraud went on for so long without being detected, despite at least one whistleblower's repeated attempts to convince the Securities and Exchange Commission that Madoff was engaged in fraud (The head of the SEC division assigned to monitor money managers resigned after

---

[a] McCoy, K. (2009, July 10). Madoff won't appeal sentence. *USA Today*, p. 3B.

the scandal broke). Like Madoff, many victims were also driven by greed. They seemed all too willing to believe that the fund could consistently outperform the market no matter the economic climate. Prosecutors are also trying to determine if others participated in the deceit. Bank and Hedge fund officials who steered billions to Madoff through feeder funds may have suspected or known of the fraud but kept sending money in return for high fees. There are suspicions that at least some of the 200 employees of the fund knew what was going on. Further, the Madoffs appear to be a close-knit family. Some observers find it hard to believe that Bernie's wife Ruth, his brother, and his sons (who worked in the firm's legitimate brokerage division) did not know of his illegal activities. Nevertheless, Madoff claims to have acted alone, and his guilty plea means he doesn't have to testify against anyone else.

Settling financial claims will be particularly difficult. The trustee appointed to shut down the business "unearthed a labyrinth of interrelated international funds, institutions, and entities of almost unparalleled complexity and breadth."[b] Recovered assets will only cover a small portion of the claims, and victims can only expect limited reimbursement from the Securities Investor Protection Corporation. The trustee is also trying to recover money from those who withdrew their "profits" before the investment fund collapsed. According to an attorney assisting in this effort, Madoff clients need to "share the pain" and realize that they have got "somebody else's money."[c] Those fortunate enough to cash in before the collapse are naturally reluctant to reimburse other investors.

Many victimized by Madoff will probably never recover. Not only were they swindled out of their retirement and college savings; in many cases, they were betrayed by someone they trusted. Bernie continued to betray those closest to him until the very end. Just weeks before his arrest, he convinced a longtime friend, a recent widow, to invest her entire life savings in his fund.

---

[b] McCoy, Madoff won't appeal sentence.

[c] McCoy, K. (2009, March 4). Madoff clients' lawsuits look to others for recompense. *USA Today*, p. 1B.

Discussion Probes

1. What unhealthy motivations drove Madoff to defraud investors and betray his friends?

2. Was Madoff's scheme "extraordinarily evil" as the judge claimed?

3. Was his punishment excessive? Will it deter other possible criminals?

4. Are the victims partially to blame for the success of this swindle?

5. Do you think Madoff acted alone, or did he have help from employees and/or family members?

6. Should clients who got their money out before the fund collapsed be forced to return these funds to help reimburse less fortunate investors?

7. What leadership and followership ethics lessons do you take from this case?

Recommended Approach

1. Who are the victims in the Bernie Madoff case? Share your personal stories of being cheated or swindled in purchasing a product or service.
Learning point: This is important to build ethical sensitivity for the victims in this case. Students will surely identify defrauded investors, but it is also important to identify Madoff's friends and family whose lives may have been ruined by Madoff's actions. Asking students to script their own stories of being deceived will help students develop more compassion for the people who were harmed in the case.

2. Enumerate the reasons for Bernie Madoff's ethical failure? Go through steps of ethical judgment using the SAD Formula (e.g., situation, analysis, decision) approach as explained in Chapter 4.
Learning point: This helps students evaluate the consequences of bad decisions. It is important for students to visualize the consequences of their actions as they would as business managers.

3. Generate multiple interpretations of key employees' and relatives' behavior in this case. How did they rationalize their behavior assuming they must have known of the illegal activities?

Learning point: It is important for students to realize how living in conflict over hidden secrets related to Madoff's operation most likely caused close friends and relatives to be unhappy, despite their affluent social status.

4. Analyze the ethical identity of Madoff, his employees, and his family members?

Learning point: Again students see that Madoff and his close aids may have had identity conflicts that caused them a lot of agony and tension, despite materialistic gains.

5. Discuss the questions that are already included in the case since they are helpful in going through the ethical process with its four components.

Learning point: Students practice reflection in case studies. This skill builds autonomy of judgment and social agency to society.

6. Put yourself in Madoff's shoes, and benefitting from all the hindsight of this case, had Madoff considered the consequences from the beginning, would he have taken this path of living a lie, why or why not?

Learning point: Students should discuss what Madoff would have given up, had he been an honest financial advisor—the lavish life, material possession, financial security, which he had to give up later. This point of reflection stresses the importance of the evaluation of consequences, when making career decisions.

7. Write a two-page summary responding to this question: What are the rewards of ethical motivation and why did Bernie Madoff fail to see them?

Learning point: Students do their most reflective thinking when writing papers, and it is important to have students practice reflection in case studies. This skill builds autonomy of judgment and social agency to society.

In watching the documentary, students find out that Madoff's family may also have been victims of this tragedy, since one of his sons ends up committing suicide at the aftermath of the scandal. Madoff and his wife became estranged, as well as other falling-outs with family and friends. This is an excellent case to discuss how failure of ethical judgment has resulted in ruining the lives of the people involved in this case, including Madoff and his family.

This type of case encourages students to reflect on finding meaning in life other than the materialistic view. This case is perfectly suited for a business ethics or a management class, but regardless of the discipline, the business educator has to be able to link to elements of ethical motivation.

We presented two sample case studies in this chapter aimed at helping students develop ethical sensitivity and motivation. Educators have to pick their cases selectively to nurture students' needed skills. Understanding the goals of each case prior to teaching it in the class is an important piece of our approach. We recommend that an educator think through the "Ethical Process Model" as they prepare for discussion of case studies. We also recommend assessing the success of the stimulation of the ethical components at the end of each class, in order to address or uncover weaknesses of the course.

Ethical Action and Giving Voice to Values Platform

Ethical action is the last, and most important, step in following through on a business or personal decision in a situation. If students, as preprofessionals, have a healthy sense of ethical sensitivity, it will be difficult for them to ignore or disregard an ethical problem around them. Ethical motivation allows them to process their personal goals and loyalties in a situation, and proceed to act based on a cultivated conscious and an ethical identity. Once students reach the ethical decision stage, educators need to reinforce students' ability to act on their decisions successfully. Mary Gentile in *Giving Voice to Values* has outlined an excellent approach for professionals to act on their values, once they have reached an ethical decision stage that needs to be implemented.[11] Her approach harnesses important points such as the following:

- Taking initiative and finding one's voice in group conversations
- Cultivating one's courage by scripting the argument and practicing it
- Collecting the relevant facts for the issue at hand
- Reframing the problem from different angles with different external views

- Enlisting allies prior to attempting to voice one's concern
- Sequencing the audiences strategically to insure success
- Selecting the timing and the approach of arguing issues

All these steps contribute to the act of ethical action. Using Gentile's approach in the classroom has facilitated ethical actions by students in our classroom. We attribute this success to the following reasons:

Gentile uses a common sense approach and makes ethics accessible to everyone without an in-depth knowledge of ethical philosophies. Her approach allows a protagonist to take an ethical situation where they have sensed inequity or unfairness (e.g., ethical sensitivity) and provides them with techniques to address it. Using the beginning assumptions in her book, students immediately feel that they share at least some of these enabling beliefs, which gives them a boost of courage. Also, her approach—asking the protagonists to start by knowing "what is the right thing to do in a situation"—calls on them to examine the case at hand, and address it with courage using the techniques provided. Gentile's short case studies and her focus on "how to get the right thing done" enables students to view ethical positions as more feasible. In addition, her suggested approach to employ collaborative peer-coaching role play, rather than an adversarial one, creates more synergies in the classroom.

Gentile's approach diverts from the practice of a "must learn ethical philosophies" approach to implement ethical action. In fact, she observed that what hinders people from acting in ethical situations is not their lack of knowledge of ethical philosophies, but rather the techniques for ethical action. In addition, Gentile notes that people underestimate their ability to script a good argument, obtain support from others in the workplace, or frame the situation to create different understanding of the problem.

It is important to note that Gentile's method is an important component of the foundation course, as well as the integrative glue in other business courses. The AACSB noted that teaching students steps for ethical action and showing them an effective process for moral courage in the work place is a much-needed element in business practice.[12] Our experience with *Giving Voice to Values* has been very positive with students. Like many others who have used GVV, student evaluations report a lasting influence from this component.

Reasons for Ethical Sensitivity before Ethical Action and Fink's Model

Our approach for establishing a foundation of ethics requires understanding the four elements that encompass an ethical process: ethical sensitivity, ethical motivation, ethical judgment, and finally ethical action. We have stressed ethical sensitivity and motivation in this chapter, in part because many business faculties do focus on ethical action, especially relative to case studies. And there are excellent resources about ethical actions, notably *Giving Voice to Values* that we discussed above.

Pascarella and Terenzini suggested that the capacity for empathy with others represents a major factor in the development of individuals to reach higher moral levels.[13] Rest, in his book *Moral Development in the Profession,* showed that business students in particular score lower on being empathetic relative to other college students.[14] They suggest that business students may have less of an opportunity to engage in the emphatic prerequisite that is necessary for growth in moral judgment. To improve this, they recommend that a *deliberate psychological education*, which emphasizes social role taking, that can be employed in the classroom, but also as a purposeful tool to engage students in their communities. Social role taking is a method where students can be placed in real roles that require empathy and disciplined listening. It has shown that students can improve in their abilities of moral development.[15]

The focus on ethical action in business ethics texts is problematic, since students would be more likely to focus on the current laws that may apply without an examination of the issues. The long-term objective is to graduate professionals who examine, interpret, empathize, frame, and reframe situations, in order to arrive at the proper ethical action. The business discipline is naturally "expertise focused" and not "judgment focused." It is different from law, social work, or psychology, where students by the nature of their discipline dig deeper below the surface to analyze issues. Yet, business students become business managers, who face ethical dilemmas needing decisions. Thus, it is imperative that students learn ethical sensitivity before moving to the other elements. Using Kohlberg's and Rest's models of ethical development—from preconventional, conventional, and postconventional phases—we would argue that ethical action is more likely if students have gone through and understood these phases. Otherwise, students may remain at the preconventional level, which the Rest model describes as being obedient to established laws in order to avoid punishment and to meet the person's interest.[16] However, if we as faculty in business schools attempt to develop students' ethical sensitivity, judgment, and motivation, we then insure a higher success of ethical action. Rest and Narvaez also recommend using components of business courses to encourage students to be active in helping disadvantaged communities.[17] This approach provides students with the experience of empathy, without giving up their hopes to become entrepreneurs and earn a profit. Another example is to have business students help nonprofits apply for grants and participate in the fund raising for organizations.

Another final framework that supports our proposed approach of building a foundation of ethics is Fink's taxonomy of significant learning, which is explained below.

Fink's Taxonomy of Significant Learning

Fink's taxonomy of significant learning is another helpful framework that supports the suggested processes in the last two chapters.[18] Since we are looking for significant change in building a foundation for an ethical process, we find that this model is helpful and consistent with our suggested approaches in Chapters 4 and 5. Significant learning occurs in a six-part taxonomy as follows: [19]

Foundational Knowledge

This part deals with acquiring the knowledge or the key concepts pertaining to a subject. For example, students acquire in-depth knowledge of important concepts in ethics. Note that this is the first component of "significant learning."

Application

This part deals with applying foundational knowledge, and comparing and contrasting opposing positions to reach decisions about appropriate methods. For example, after students learn the foundational knowledge of ethics, then they begin to apply it in the cases included in the different subjects of business.

Integration

This part deals with connecting ideas and applying them in different contexts. For example, students will be able to frame ethical situations and apply different ethical philosophies to fit the situation at hand.

Human Dimension

This part deals with reflection on knowledge learned. Students will be able to use their team members for brainstorming and feedback, learning about themselves in the process. For example, discussing case studies in class shows different perspectives, thus influencing students' opinions.

Caring

This part deals with developing new views, feelings, and values. Upon the integration of knowledge due to the steps above, students start to care enough to want to apply correct principles to life events. For example, once students understand the impact of pollution on the environment, they will care enough to select hybrid cars in their auto purchases. This is similar to ethical motivation in the Narvaez and Lies model.[20]

Learning How to Learn

This part deals with the continuing desire to learn about the topic, thus becoming a self-learner. For example, once students understand the impact of ethics on their professionalism, they will continue reading and researching about the topic.

Fink shows the process when significant student learning happens in the classroom. This model of "significant learning" has key importance in building and nurturing a foundation for ethical action in students. This is another confirmation that in order to influence ethical behavior of these preprofessionals, educators must follow a process.[21]

Conclusion

Fink highlights the notion that a foundational knowledge is important for "significant learning."[22] Also, the application of knowledge is another key element resulting in integration of knowledge and the application. We consider the teaching of ethics in different business courses as the "application and integration" step in Fink's model. The fourth through sixth elements in Fink's model are elements that we foresee happening in the classroom as educators discuss cases and ask students to engage with and listen to one another. The last element in the model "learning how to learn" is one of research and reflection. Educators should always give assignments asking students to research and reflect.

In the last two chapters, we presented what we believe are important methods for helping business students gain lasting knowledge of the ethical process. We hope that the AACSB, business schools, business deans, and educators make room in the business curriculum for such learning that will surely lead to increasing ethical actions.

Notes

1. Ward (1970).
2. Gentile (2010); Piper, Gentile and Parks (1993); Trank and Rynes (2003).
3. Khurana (2007); Schein (1972).
4. Brint (1996).
5. Rest (1984).
6. Narvaez and Endicott (2009); Narvaez and Bock (2009); Narvaez and Lies (2009).
7. Narvaez and Endicott (2009); Narvaez and Bock (2009); Narvaez and Lies (2009).
8. Johnson (2016), pp. 398–99.
9. Johnson (2013), pp. 71–73.
10. Smith Martin, *The Madoff Affair (2009)*.
11. Gentile (2010).
12. AACSB (2003).
13. Pascarella and Terenzini (1991).
14. Rest and Narvaez (1994).

15. Rest and Narvaez (1994).
16. Rest (1984).
17. Rest (1994).
18. Fink (2013).
19. Fink (2013).
20. Narvaez and Lies (2009).
21. Fink (2013).
22. Fink (2013).

PART 4

Suggested Curricular Path Towards Professionalism

CHAPTER 6

Achieving the Goals of Multi-disciplinary Thinking

. . . Humanities have been delineated by Ronald S. Crane (1886–1967) as the cultivation of four essential "arts: language, analysis of ideas, literary and artistic criticism, and historiography." . . . Humanities scholarship and education are dedicated to understanding human experience through the disciplined development of insight, perspective, critical understanding, discernment, and creativity.

—Cole, et al.[1]

Keywords

Business education, higher education, multi-frame thinking, theory in the business curriculum, research, critical thinking, interdisciplinary collaboration

Introduction

Imagine a first-year student who is sure she wants to major in business. She does not yet see the connections between her passion for economics and business finance and the general education courses that she is required to take. One of these requirements is that a cohort of first-year students enrolls in a writing seminar linked to another course. Looking at the options, she selects the "Literature of the Great Depression." To her surprise, she finds that the literature course focuses on the impacts of the Depression on families much like hers. She becomes more interested in the connections between economic decisions and people's lives.

During her second year, she takes a business elective that examines the importance of ethical decision-making for managers. After this course, she chooses to take a philosophy course on ethics. She is learning a lot about different perspectives. Even though she does not want to be a manager, she is required to take "Management and Organizational Behavior," a course that helps her understand that being able to understand different perspectives is at the core of good management. She also has been involved in co-curricular activities, and decides she wants to be a Residential Assistant—which leads her to take "Foundations of Leadership." In this course, she again is exposed to how so many perspectives—including literature, art, philosophy, history—can contribute to understanding and practicing leadership. This combination of multidisciplinary coursework and activities parallels some of the recommendations made in *Rethinking Undergraduate Business Education: Liberal Learning for the Profession:*

> Students need the insights of psychology, sociology, anthropology, and humanities fields as history, politics, literature, and ethics in order to develop the disciplined perspective they will need as future business persons who can grasp their shifting responsibilities and be prepared to respond quickly to new contexts.[2] (p. 48)

The Need for Multi-disciplinary Thinking

Taking the range of courses suggested by Colby et al. (and others) is important for students. But many are never asked to reflect on how humanities courses or concepts connect to business. In the example above, our student's commitment to economics and finance as "king" was challenged as she learned about their impacts on families. Our student was taught to master the use of multiple perspectives in both her general education and business courses. She studied ethics from both philosophical and business perspectives. But how do we help students to integrate multiple perspectives and use them in decision-making?

Nancy Adler's examination of the role of the arts in teaching management and leadership offers some of the most compelling answers to this question. In her article "Finding Beauty in a Fractured World: Art Inspires Leaders—Leaders Change the World," she asks: "Given the power of analytic understanding—driven as it is to claim life as *knowable*—how do we re-recognize the *unknowable?*"[3] (p. 480) She urges us to see and use science and art as partners that provide different lenses. In her artistic work, as well as in research, teaching, and consulting, her use of both lenses provides specific examples of the ways that art:

- "gives us back the capacity to perceive uniqueness"
- supports the "ability to see what is unique within the context of that which is comfortably familiar"
- can change perspectives, as one paints or views from different angles
- can see reality more clearly (Pp. 484–87)

In this same article, Adler describes a study done at Yale Medical School that compared medical students who took art history with those who did not.[4] She reports that:

> . . . Researchers discovered that the art-trained students' diagnostic skills improved significantly more than did the skills of their non-art trained colleagues. . . . [They] learned how to see but also gained a deeper appreciation of the relative nature of interpretation. . . . [They] saw more of what they were looking for, and more important, more of what they were not looking for. . . . They were more aware . . . that their diagnoses were best guesses . . . .[5] (p. 487)

The groundbreaking book *Can Ethics Be Taught? Perspectives, Challenges, and Approaches at Harvard Business School* offers more evidence of the value of multiple perspectives. In this, Parks cites the work of Rest to argue that: "there is now ample evidence that ethical consciousness and commitment can continue to undergo transformation at least throughout formal education."[6] She urges that business curricula can be designed to both engage students in multiple perspectives and ethical decision-making. In so doing, students can hone their abilities to tolerate complexity, cultivate diverse points of view, and combine rigorous analysis and informed imagination. Parks argues that:

> First, these students need to be given opportunities for active, critical reflection upon the circumstances and opportunities before them. Second, they must be encouraged to become more active agents, most immediately in the present context of their own educational process.[7] (p. 58)

In Chapter 3 of the same text, Gentile examines how faculties are central to this process, not only in terms of the courses they teach and the overall business curriculum, but also:

> In order . . . to have the hoped-for broad and long-term impact on the school and its curriculum, ethical analysis and values-based decision making [has] to be the subject of new empirical research, decision-model building, and case study and course development across the whole curriculum. (p. 73).

Combining the conclusions of Parks and Gentile, one important way to connect both faculty and students to these endeavors is through undergraduate research. In particular, community-based undergraduate research is an important tool to help strengthen business students' commitments to ethical decision-making (see Chapter 8). As noted by Elizabeth L. Paul, such engagement can involve:

> . . . Engagement in real contexts; engagement in real-world complexities and ambiguities; work directed toward the accomplishment of real and meaningful goals; side-by-side collaboration between 'novices' and 'experts'; and ongoing opportunity for feedback, discussion, and reflection.[8] (p. 198)

So what changes does this imply for business curricula? The challenge is highlighted in *Rethinking Undergraduate Business Education.*[9] Colby and her colleagues stress the importance of critical questioning, but suggest that business faculty see the syllabus as already too full. As one stated: "presenting business as an object of inquiry and critical questioning cannot be the central goal of the course, given how full the syllabus is already." (p. 37) However, the authors go on to suggest that "an additional, linked experience" could provide an opportunity for critical questioning. Building on their advice, we have chosen to use texts, films, and case studies that help students learn not only business concepts and practices but also the theories and research that inform decision-making. Our commitment is that students are immersed in:

- Interdisciplinary learning/teaching multiple frames
- Development of critical thinking skills

- Understanding the importance of theory development and research
- Collaboration with others across disciplines

The vignette at the beginning of this chapter illustrates many of the suggestions that follow but also makes clear the importance of consistent reinforcement of learning, understanding, and practicing our goals. The remainder of the chapter describes approaches that can facilitate these goals. They range from what can be done by a single faculty member, to extensive collaboration in team-taught or linked courses.

Teaching Multi-disciplinary Thinking

We begin with one of the staples of an undergraduate business major, namely, a course on the management of business organizations. Faculty who teach these courses select from a range of options; our choice has been texts and case studies that introduce students to multiple perspectives. Ideally, the core of the course teaches students to use multiple perspectives, engage in critical thinking, understand the theories of and research about management and leadership, and explore the concept and practice of collaboration. These understandings and skills will help them as they explore case studies about, conflict among, and decisions to be made by managers of organizations.

The case studies that we use are often designed for students at the graduate level (such as those from Harvard Business School Publishing). The goal is NOT to overwhelm the students with the details of the case. Rather, we ask students to find illustrations of the concepts that they are studying and to make recommendations based on course readings. Many of the cases we use are more historic in nature for two reasons: first, they provide students with a glance at the recent past; and second, they encourage students to examine what happened after the case study. The following are examples of texts and case studies used in teaching a course that deals with management and organizational behavior. Each of the three books used provides support for several of our learning goals, although the following discussions focus on the primary contribution(s) of each publication.

Multi-frame Thinking

A text such as Lee G. Bolman and Terrence E. Deal's *Reframing Organizations: Artistry, Choice and Leadership* provides the background that students need to understand different perspectives and engage in dialog with others who have different points of view.[10] The authors use the concept of four frames—structural, human resources, political, and symbolic—to describe organizations. Since the research they examine draws from the disciplinary perspectives of sociology, social psychology, political science, anthropology, theatre, and more, students may recognize ideas that they learned in other courses. In addition, the authors discuss many examples to help students understand that the best managers are facile with multiple—and sometimes contradictory—perspectives. Bolman and Deal's approach grounds the study of management in many fields, and provides students with the language and concepts of frames that can be used in exploring and analyzing case studies. Those case studies provide "real world" examples that students can use to "practice" their analytical skills from multiple or interdisciplinary perspectives.

For the *structural frame*, students read two case studies: *GlaxoSmith-Kline: Reorganizing Drug Discovery (A)*[11] and *Wyeth Pharmaceuticals: Spurring Scientific Creativity with Metrics*.[12] Each case deals with how that pharmaceutical company restructured the work of their scientists relative to the development of new drugs (see below regarding module that introduces students to the process of drug approval). Using concepts and examples from Bolman and Deal, we ask students to analyze each organizational structure prior to and after reorganization. We then ask students to think about what was left out or not considered—this usually leads to a discussion of human resources, which is the next frame studied in the course.

To illustrate the *human resources* frame, the classic example used is *Human Resources at Hewlett Packard (A)*.[13] First, we ask students to describe the structure of groups at HP and then compare them with the pharmaceutical case studies. This leads into a discussion of what was different at HP, the "HP Way," with its focus on small, decentralized work groups and policies that encouraged both teamwork and individual innovation. Because this case illustrates human resources policies, the reward system, management practices, and the importance of symbols and culture, it helps students understand the importance of using all four frames.

For the *political frame*, students examine a case that is about both power and gender. *Ann Hopkins (A)* takes place during a time when few women were partners in firms such as Price Waterhouse.[14] Students often focus on the personal strengths and weaknesses of Hopkins, who was described as someone who yelled, used profanity, was "tough" and arrogant, showed disrespect for subordinates, and had a hard-driving style. Many see these characteristics as reasons why she was not selected to be a partner. We encourage students to examine the selection process closely and the comments made by those evaluating Hopkins. While the focus of the discussion is on both formal and informal power, we also explore gender issues. Because this case includes issues that are also symbolic in nature, it helps to introduce students to Bolman and Deal's fourth frame and provides a transition to the final "case study" Shakespeare's *Henry V.*

We use *Henry V* to examine the symbolic frame. Because it deals with war, we challenge students to set aside the political frame and concentrate on the importance of rituals, myths, speeches, celebrations, . . . and other types of symbols and their meanings. In teaching this case, faculty in the humanities developed some assignments. One approach uses Shakespeare's text, another uses Kenneth Branagh's film *Henry* V, and the third involves a theatre workshop (see below for description) focused on Henry V's "St. Crispin's Day Speech." Bolman and Deal's concepts (myths, vision, values, stories, rituals, ceremony, and/or metaphor (found in Chapter 12 of their book) guide the discussions for all three modules.

Infusing Theory into the Curriculum

While case studies provide students with real-life examples, we believe that it is essential that business students wrestle with the theories and research that informs actual business practices. While it is clear that they are taught these in the field of economics, other social sciences often are not included within business courses. Thus, a second important element of Bolman and Deal's *Reframing Organizations* is that it examines theory and research from a range of the social sciences disciplines. Each of the four frames is examined using highly respected researchers, theorists, leaders, and authors, both classical and contemporary (e.g., ranging from Aristotle to Argyris, Buddha to Bass, and so on through the alphabet).

Because Bolman and Deal weave together theories, research results, and examples for each frame, students begin to see the consequences of using different frames in different situations. Students begin to understand that management is steeped in the social sciences and the humanities. Finally, woven through their text are examples of a range of ethical choices (developed more fully in their text *The Wizard and the Warrior*).[15] The chapter "Reframing Ethics and Spirit" provides examples, framing, and ideas, giving opportunities for faculty to engage students in such discussions.

Understanding the Importance of Research and Theory Development

The next text is Rosabeth Moss Kanter's *Supercorp: How Vanguard Companies Create Innovation, Profits, Growth, and Social Good*.[16] She illustrates how many companies have successfully resolved the seeming contradiction of economics and ethical decision-making. Grounded in more than 3 years of research, the work examines large multinational corporations that have found a way to contribute to communities and do well financially. As she states in the Introduction: "IBM . . . Proctor and Gamble, Banco Real, and Publicis Groupe . . . have achieved the seemingly impossible: high levels of business performance—innovation, growth, and profit—and social good."(p. 1)

Kanter's work also provides a global perspective, arguing that companies that are more global in nature need to make deep connections at both local and national levels. This means connections not only with business partners but also with officials in certain parts of the government, public individuals who can serve as intermediaries, and community organizations. At the core of her book is the idea that corporations have both the know-how and the responsibility to "address some of the world's most challenging social and environmental problems." (p. 206) In her chapter "The Triumph of Transformational Enterprise: Leadership for the Future" she gives practical advice. Based on her research, she argues that:

. . . The best characteristics of leaders at all levels in vanguard companies can be distilled into the ultimate job description for the future . . .

- Intellect: Systems thinking
- Action: Initiative taker
- Relationships: Persuasion and diplomacy
- Emotion: Self-awareness and empathy
- Spirituality: Values driven[17] (p. 261)

Not only are these important elements of leadership, they provide students with concepts that often are learned in the study of the humanities—especially self-awareness, empathy, spirituality, and motivation rooted in values. As we have noted, self-concept, ethical behavior, and concern for the wider community/social agency are at the core of professionalism. Many of Kanter's chapters offer examples of corporations that illustrate these professional characteristics. When we focus on the ethical decision-making of those in the organizations, we use them as mini-case studies for analysis and discussion, especially the five characteristics listed above. In addition, we require students to write a four-page paper that looks in depth at one of the corporate examples. They do further research about the organization and discuss their findings through the lens of Kanter's text. In doing so, they must consider the professional elements of both expertise and social-trusteeship.

Critical Thinking and Collaboration

A final text that is often used in management courses is Peter Senge's *The Fifth Discipline: The Art and Practice of a Learning Organization.*[18] Like Bolman and Deal's work, Senge focuses on the multiple, and often conflicting, points of view which need to be brought into decision-making. At the core of Senge's work is the importance of mastering five concepts: "systems thinking, personal mastery, mental models, building shared vision, and team learning." Senge's ideas are rooted in his study of those who used those five concepts successfully.

"Systems thinking" is essential to understanding how organizations work, especially how decisions and actions are interrelated. That approach requires analysis of the various elements of an organization—structure, policies, culture, power—as well as an understanding of the sum and connections of its parts, the external environment, and how they all interact. Although these are fairly complex ideas for undergraduates, Senge provides negative examples (Chapter 4 "The Laws of the Fifth Discipline") that introduce students to some of the concepts that are part of the core disciplines discussed in "The Core Disciplines: Building the Learning Organization."

"Personal mastery" focuses on the individual. It refers to the imperative that individuals in an organization need to engage in learning new competences and skills in ways that Senge describes as "approaching one's life as creative work." We need to be clear about what we value on the one hand and learn to face reality on the other. As Senge notes:

> The juxtaposition of vision (what we want) and a picture of current reality (where we are relative to what we want) generates . . . 'creative tension' . . . The essence on personal mastery is learning how to generate and sustain creative tension in our lives.[19] (p. 132)

"Mental models" are the generalizations, ideas, assumptions, hopes, images, and theories that shape how each of us interprets our lives and experiences with others. Like stereotypes, they are deeply ingrained and usually what influences our actions. Senge and others encourage managers and their teams to share their mental models. By bringing these models to the surface and scrutinizing them, teams engage in institutional learning (Pp. 163–64). We reinforce this concept by asking students to identify their own mental models by exploring personal assumptions, hopes, and theories.

This process of discovery is essential to building a "shared vision" . . . "not an idea . . . [but in Senge's words] rather, a force in people's hearts." (p. 193) By sharing the deepest thoughts, different groups who hold very different ideas may uncover obscured commonalities.

Sharing goals, values, and mission supports the final core discipline of "team learning." Senge makes the point that unlike discussion, team learning requires genuine dialogue during which "[participants] suspend their assumptions but they may communicate their assumptions freely." (p. 224) To do so requires careful listening and speaking to avoid patterns of interaction such as defensiveness.

It is important to have students study these ideas and examples, and perhaps more importantly, practice them in class, in their roles on campus, and as they work in teams on the final class assignment. In the process, they also reinforce the importance of several elements of professionalism. Examining personal goals and realities, assessing personal mastery, and exploring personal mental models, certainly impacts self-concept. Senge's emphasis on team learning supports a sense of expertise; shapes autonomy of judgment, and helps clarifies what it means to be professional. The case study described below provides good and bad examples of Senge's disciplines.

The single case study used with the Senge text is "San Diego Padres: PETCO Park as a Catalyst for Urban Redevelopment."[20] As the title suggests, PETCO Park was a massive undertaking that involved many different groups with wildly different goals. These included everything from the city of San Diego, the Major League Baseball Padres, the National Trust for Historic Places and local services for the homeless and families who might use the park. We ask students to return to the case study multiple times. After reading Senge's chapter on a core discipline, students search the case study for examples. After finishing the Senge text, students write a five-page analysis of the Padres' case, applying what they have learned about Senge's disciplines.

In looking back at the texts and cases discussed, it bears repeating that while the authors use different examples, theories, approaches, and terms, they all require that students understand and practice multiple perspectives. To further expand students' thinking beyond the management of organizations, we have taken the important step of collaborating with colleagues in the arts and humanities and integrating their points of view into the business administration curriculum.

Interdisciplinary Collaborative Approaches

A second way to bring the liberal arts into a business course is through collaboration with a faculty member with expertise in such fields as literature, philosophy, and history, all disciplines that explore the ethics of decision-making. These collaborations range from developing modules to team teaching.

Modules

We ask colleagues to build a module, namely, a class discussion or lecture that shares their expertise about the topic under study. These modules create a tangible "product," a concrete strategy with support materials that business faculty members can use in their future teaching. A typical class session(s) builds on a course reading, novel, or film, and engages students in discussion or debate. The "product" might include slides, clips from a film or news story, lecture notes, discussion questions, debates, and the like. While a module is designed for a particular course, it may be suitable for other courses as well. While a module is only a small part of a course, it can have a powerful impact, especially if it illustrates multiple perspectives and encourages discussions of ethical decision-making. The following describes some of the modules that were developed, organized for specific kinds of business courses.

Courses That Focus on Management and Organizations

- Abraham Lincoln's leadership: Assign the film *Lincoln* (2012) with instructions to look for such elements as the "frames" Lincoln used, and the ways in which ethical decision-making, actions, and the like were evident or not. [21] Class discussion also includes two modules developed in collaboration with a historian. These focus on the many decisions that Lincoln made earlier in his Presidency. One module focuses on Lincoln's choices for members of his first Cabinet, namely that he selected members he felt were the most qualified to accomplish the tasks of their position, regardless of personal grievances with him or other Cabinet members. Another focuses on the way Lincoln handled the Union Army, with special attention on General George B. McClellan.[22] Both of these modules also could be used in courses focused on leadership.
- Shakespeare's *Henry V*: Several modules use *Henry V*. In one module developed by Jonathan Burton (English), students read Shakespeare's text. Another module uses the film *Henry V* (1989) starring Kenneth Branagh.[23] Both explore the

complexity of leading/managing, as well as the ethical nature of the king's decisions. The following describes a module developed by Gil Gonzalez (Theatre) in which students participate in a theatre workshop using Henry V's "St. Crispin's Day" speech. Workshop activities—using various voices, "walking the speech," and reciting it in contorted physical positions—focus student attention on the words, rhythms, and implications of the speech that lead him to leadership. One of the unexpected benefits is that, by the end of the workshop, there is an increased sense of community and a deeper understanding that using multiple perspectives is important for managers and leaders. This module ends with an assignment to view the whole film and write an analysis of Shakespeare's interpretation of *Henry V* as a leader.

Courses on Management/Leadership That Introduce Students to Multiple Ways of Looking at Leadership

- Using Niall Ferguson's *Civilization: The West and the Rest*,[24] Natale Zappia (History) developed a module for the course "A Tale of Two Cities: Doing Business in Hong Kong and China." Students studied Ferguson's "six powerful new concepts . . . [of] competition, science, property rights, medicine, consumerism, and work ethic" that helped explain the domination of the West. Students then engaged in a contemporary analysis of current cultural and geopolitical realities and discussed whether the days of Western global leadership are numbered.
- Historian Laura McEnaney developed a module that examines the question: "How did social movements in the 1960s (both) experiment with and redefine leadership?" Focusing on the civil rights movement and second-wave feminism, the module illustrated how historians view leadership and asked students to compare this to their current understanding of leadership. Based on the readings[25], students were asked questions and engaged in discussions about leadership as a liberal art.

Courses in Finance and Accounting

- For the course "Business Research Methods," Michelle Chihara (English) developed a module on the use of qualitative research methods. Building a narrative around Malcolm Gladwell's "The Science of Shopping," the module described the ideas of Paco Underhill.[26] He used observations and videotapes as qualitative research about women's shopping and developed "a retailing commandment: a women's product that requires extensive examination should never be placed in a narrow aisle." His explanation was that, should a woman be brushed against, she would move away from the product she was examining.
- Some of the most challenging modules were for the required course "Business Finance" (taught by Fatos Radoniqi). Irfana Hashmi (Religious Studies) developed two modules that explored the history, religion, and culture that influences Islamic finance and law. The first module used selections from Frank Vogel's "Islamic Finance as the Application of Islamic Law" and provided students with an introduction to Islamic finance.[27] The second module provided an overview of the political economy of the Middle East in the medieval and early modern eras, based on a conference paper given by Sevket Pamuk.[28] For students who wanted to learn more, an additional reading was suggested.[29] (As an aside, we found "Usury and Just Compensation: Religious and Financial Ethics in Historical Perspective" very interesting. As the authors state: "By re-examining past ethical discussions of the distinction between usury and just compensation, we argue that the world's religious traditions can make significant contributions to contemporary debate.")[30] (p. 10)
- Lana Nino (Business) revised "Principles of Financial Accounting" to include a film documentary *The Corporation*[31] that critically examines the history of the expansion of corporate powers. A second reading by Douglas Beets "Critical Events in the Ethics of U.S. Corporation History"

summarizes the evolution of corporations from the mid-1700s to the present.[32] After reflecting on this history and the critique from the documentary, students were asked to make their recommendations for the next phase of corporate structure.

- In "Principles of Managerial Accounting," Nino added a module using the book entitled, *Conscious Capitalism, With a New Preface by the Authors: Liberating the Heroic Spirit of Business*[33] and an article "The Long History of Conscious Capitalism: A response to James O'Toole and David Vogel's 'Two and a half cheers for conscious capitalism.'" By reading *Conscious Capitalism*, students learned to look for the "higher purpose" of organizations, and how companies can join their profit goals with their societal ones. While applying managerial accounting concepts to an analysis of a corporation, students also learned to look for the possible "higher purpose" and how they can benefit society.

Courses That Deal with Ethics

- Paul Kjellberg (Philosophy) developed a module about Confucian leadership for a course that explored ethical issues faced by managers and leaders. In addition, he prepared a module on Buddhism, meditation, and innovation for a class that dealt with innovation.
- A module on Richard Nixon's presidency, developed by historian Laura McEnaney, explored the complexity of human nature, ethical decision-making, and unethical decisions that sometimes have ethical impacts. Students prepared for the class with two readings: James T. Patterson, *Grand Expectations: The United States, 1945–1974*, Chapter 25, "End of an Era: Expectations amid Watergate and Recession" and Barbara Kellerman, *Bad Leadership: What It Is, How It Happens, Why It Matters*, Chapters 1 to 3.[34] During class, students examined the timeline of events, watched a video, and responded to a list of discussion questions.

Courses Dealing with International Business and Marketing

- Luz Maria Galbraith (director of the Cultural Center) developed modules that dealt with the histories and cultures of Latin America. The intent was to help students taking International Marketing understand histories and challenges of the region. Beginning with an overview that provided both an introduction to Mexico and a short discussion of NAFTA, one module then focused on a brief history of Mexico and its social institutions, especially political and economic. It examined culture in terms of family, social class, nationalism, aesthetic expressions, rituals, and traditions. The second module focused on the middle class in Latin America by discussing income, poverty levels, economic mobility, education, migration, social class, and status.
- Environmental scientist Cinzia Fissore developed several class sessions for a business course on sustainable development. One module examined the declining food production in Africa, which is due to the decline in the quality of the land resource base. Students studied the role that soil plays in globalization and sustainable development. Because soil quality means the ability of the soil to perform its functions in a sustainable manner, the potential for growing depends on land management and correct use of very different types of soils that range from prime to low potential. As Natasha Gilbert states: "The key to tackling hunger in Africa is enriching its soil. The big debate is about how to do it."[35] (p. 1) A second module used two readings, "Feeding the World: Disappearing Land" from the World Resources Institute and "African agriculture: Dirt poor," which focus on land and land degradation around the world. [36]

Collaborations Across the Disciplines

For colleges/universities with a curriculum that supports collaboration across disciplines, there are more extensive possibilities to focus on

multi-disciplinary teaching and encourage learning via multiple perspectives and critical questioning and thinking. As Colby, et al. suggest: "Perhaps then, business programs need to provide an additional, linked experience that could enable students, as citizens of the world, to focus squarely on the purposes, relationships, or responsibilities of business or of their business lives."[37] (p. 37) One of the basic ways to do this is to have students co-enroll in two or more courses that present different perspectives, as described in the beginning of this chapter. While this model provides a kind of learning community, students are usually left to make the connections between ideas studied in each of the courses. There is another option that provides students with greater multi-disciplinary connections. Like co-enrollment, students take two paired courses, but the two faculty members are more involved in each other's courses. They attend and participate in the linked course, serving as master learners. In addition, there is at least one common major assignment that requires students to integrate the perspectives of both courses. While these so-called "pairs" can be taught as lower- or upper-level courses, the following examples were designed for more advanced students.

The first course "Humanistic Values in Management" (Lana Nino, Business Administration) was paired with "Documentary Film Movements and Genres" (John Bak, Film Studies) to explore film documentaries and the study of business ethics. The course in business emphasizes the importance of values in making organizations and commerce work. It encourages students to move beyond a singular utilitarian focus to adopt a broader perspective on human needs. It also encourages students to analyze ethical issues using theoretical frameworks and express their views based on informed theory and common practices. The film course examines the history of documentary filmmaking viewed through subject matter dealing with multiple examples of leadership both ethical and unethical. Films included *Harlan County USA* (Kopple), *Triumph of the Will* (Riefenstahl), *Fog of War* (Morris), and docudramas such as *Frost/Nixon* (Howard) and *Margin Call* (Chandor).[38] The films' subjects complement the topics covered in the business course for each week and help lead students to a deeper understanding of the material in both courses.

A second example pairs "Sustainable Development and the Triple Bottom Line" (Daniel Duran, Business) with "Soils and Environmental

Geomorphology" (Cinzia Fissore, Environmental Science). It focuses on the role and impact of renewable portfolio management, energy conservation, water policy, and waste treatment that support socially responsible economic development and their geomorphological impacts on the earth's crust. The course included field trips aimed at helping students see the connections at the core of the pair. Responses to a Learning Impact Questionnaire reveal very positive feedback on the pair's contribution to: examining environmental values and issues in the students' own culture and other cultures; examining personal values and impact on the environment; enriching students' understanding of their major through exposure to other fields; and analyzing topics from multiple fields and perspectives.

The concept of paradigm shift is often applied to many areas to examine significant change. The course "Paradigm Shifts in the Arts" (Jennifer Holmes, Theatre) was paired with "Theories and Practices of Leadership" (Susan Gotsch, Sociology). Students study such shifts in art, music, theatre, film, management practices, leadership theories, social movements, as well as the historical influences that contributed to change. The courses reinforce the importance of having a strong interdisciplinary mindset and focuses students' attention on the commonalities that encourage creative thinking and innovation.

Other Pairs Combined

- "Financial Crisis," with a focus on the institutional history of crises (Fatos Radoniqi, Business Administration), with the literature course: "Bubbles, Plots, and Panics: The Literature and Culture of Financial Crises"(Michelle Chihara, English)
- "Tragedy of the Commons" (David Bourgaize, Biology) with "Social Media Marketing" (Kristin Smirnov, Business Administration)
- "Managing Creativity and Innovation" (developed by Jessica Federman, Business Administration) with "Early Chinese Philosophy" (Paul Kjellberg, Philosophy)

Students can learn important lessons in these paired courses, lessons that go beyond just learning about a nonbusiness subject. A pair might address ethics and social responsibility by watching and discussing documentary films that illustrate a variety of personal and corporate behaviors. In the paradigm shift course described above, students made historical connections between the changes in the arts and the shifts that occurred in business. Pairing a course in financial issues with literature provides the kind of learning described in the opening vignette of this chapter. In all of these courses, students are exposed to different perspectives, alternate ways to look at the same issue. They see solutions emerge from other disciplines. They watch strategies emerge from expertise outside their own experience. The common projects required by the paired courses demonstrate the value of collaboration. Dialogue in the innovative arena of ideas hones interpersonal, communication, and listening skills. If successful, eyes and minds open to context beyond the traditional world of business and business leadership. The next step in solidifying and institutionalizing this approach to business education could be to develop courses in leadership that would appeal to students from multiple majors. Chapter 7 focuses on the importance of business students gaining an understanding of leadership and on the development of several courses that support this.

Notes

1. Cole, Carlin, and Carson (2014, p. 3).
2. Colby, Ehrlich, Sullivan, and Dolle (2011).
3. Adler (2015).
4. Dolev, Friedlaender, & Braverman (2001).
5. Adler (2015).
6. Piper, Gentile, and Parks (1993).
7. Piper, Gentile, and Parks (1993).
8. Jacoby and Associates (2009), p. 198.
9. Colby, Ehrlich, Sullivan, and Dolle (2011).
10. Bolman and Deal (2013).
11. Huckman & Strick (2007).
12. Huckman, Pisano, and Rennella (2007).
13. Beer and Rogers (1995).
14. Badaracco and Barkan (2001).
15. Bolman and Deal (2006).

16. Kanter (2009).
17. Kanter (2009).
18. Senge (2006).
19. Senge (2006).
20. Davila, Foster, and Hoyt (2008).
21. *Lincoln* (2012).
22. Maciariello and Linkletter (2011).
23. *Henry V* (1989).
24. Ferguson (2011).
25. Gordon (2002).
26. Gladwell (1996).
27. Vogel (1998).
28. Pamuk (2010).
29. http://www.washingtonpost.com/wp-dyn/content/article/2008/05/12/AR2008051202740.html
30. Mews and Abraham (2007).
31. *The Corporation* (2003).
32. Beets (2011).
33. Mackey and Sisodia (2014).
34. Patterson (1996); Kellerman (2004).
35. Gilbert (2012).
36. World Resources Institute (2012); Gilbert (2012).
37. Colby, Ehrlich, Sullivan, and Dolle (2011).
38. *Harlan County USA* (1976); *Triumph of the Will* (1935); *Fog of War* (2003); *Frost/Nixon* (2008); *Margin Call* (2011).

CHAPTER 7

Using Leadership Approaches to Build Self-concept

Management in these cutting-edge sectors of knowledge-creation has become a form of leadership as much or more than it is the application of technical disciplines. To support innovation, business education will have to nurture mature practical judgment that can guide knowledge-intensive enterprise equitable for social benefit as well as profit.

—Colby, et al.[1]

Keywords

Organizational leadership education, higher education, self-concept, change, individual growth, societal forces, systems thinking, humanistic values

Introduction

At the core of this quote is the importance of "mature practical judgment" that supports the organization, its employees, and society. As we have pointed out in previous chapters, to do that requires the dimensions of professionalism: expertise; autonomy of thinking and of judgment; social agency; and professional self-concept. The question for this chapter is how can faculty help undergraduate business students use foundational leadership theory to develop the elements of professionalism. It is particularly important that students understand and accept that these dimensions are all necessary, and that financial performance is not the only element of a successful professional.

While there are many ways to develop self-concept, research shows that experience with diversity is an important route. As Laird stated:

> ". . . Students with more experiences with diversity, particularly enrollment in diversity courses and positive interactions with diverse peers, are more likely to score higher on academic self-confidence, social agency, and critical thinking disposition. *In addition, the study provides evidence that diversity experiences may work together to foster development of certain aspects of self.*"[2] (Emphasis added)

Thus, it is clear that professional self-concept, especially relative to moral and ethical self-concept, can be shaped by actions in classrooms—discussions, group work, case studies—that introduce students to multiple perspectives and challenge them to wrestle with ethical dilemmas.

While much has been written about whether management and leadership are the same, this chapter takes the position of the opening quote. Namely, that studying leadership, analyzing cases and situations related to leadership, and participating in leadership positions can help students build self-confidence in their abilities and a commitment to society and others, in order to lead and manage, especially in knowledge-based settings.

Chapter 6 briefly mentioned the development of courses in leadership as a next step for colleges interested in a more integrated approach to professionalism. The following discussion examines some of the literature on leadership and then provides descriptions of two courses that we have developed. Each uses approaches that contribute to the development of professional self-concept, further reinforces the use of multiple perspectives, fosters better understanding of oneself as a potential and ethical leader, and strengthens one's self-concept to do so.

Introducing Students to the Study of Leadership[a]

One of the most important lessons about leadership is to help students understand that there are a multitude of perspectives on leadership that

---

[a] We were very lucky to have Professor Jeffrey Decker as a colleague—one who had expertise in leadership and its connections to management. He was generous with his time in "coaching" us about the literature, case studies, and the like; providing

are sometimes contradictory. Our approach does not focus on the various theories or perspectives on leadership, although students are introduced to them. Rather we have selected resources that reinforce the liberal learning and help students develop a self-concept that is not just about expertise. Students need to understand that the examination of leadership dates back to ancient times, has changed somewhat through the ages, and that many contemporary leaders and leadership experts emphasize the importance of a broad liberal education.[3] This may come as a surprise to students, as their views of leadership may focus on the traits of well-known leaders. In her article "Learning Leadership Discipline by Discipline," Muhlenfeld discusses how many fields—economics, music, medicine, science, poetry, literature, and story-telling—teach students specific skills, habits, and metaphors that contribute to their leadership potentials.[4] The challenge for students is to move beyond specific discipline-related approaches to encompass the range of possibilities, namely to have a broad liberal education.

For students beginning to study leadership, it is important to explore a range of theories, studies, and experiences that help us understand leadership. Among these are looking at the individual leader, his or her followers, the nature of change, and the societal contexts.

The Individual

To look at the individual leader, one could begin by asking students to write words and/or characteristics that they think describe a leader. Students can then compare their ideas with a student from a different major to see if there is an overlap. A second activity is to engage in small-group work; for example, reading short sections about Eleanor Roosevelt (from Gardner's work).[5] Each group can then present a short oral summary of their section. Finally, each individual student then compares what they have learned about Eleanor Roosevelt's leadership relative to the words and characteristics that she or he has written, followed by a discussion. Students could also view the documentary about Grace Lee Boggs (*American Revolutionary*).[6] The importance of this introduction is obviously to

feedback on this Chapter; was crucial in generating ideas related to the grant; and served as a co-coordinator of the grant.

get students thinking about leadership, but also to challenge some of their ideas about leaders. Both Roosevelt and Boggs did not see themselves as leaders, but rather became engaged in issues that each cared about. Their leadership, as women in the 20th century, also illustrates historical contributions of women (beyond the "Joan of Arcs"). Importantly, both women were fortunate to receive an education that was steeped in the liberal arts.

This reading and the film help students make connections between a liberal arts education and leadership. This can be reinforced through such articles as Cronin's "The Liberal Arts and Leadership Learning" that introduces students to the intellectual roots of the liberal arts and explores their developmental aspects. Beginning with a discussion of leadership as performance art, he shows students how the arts of listening, speaking, debating, writing, community building, negotiation, social and emotional self-efficacy, and creativity are an essential part of successful leadership.[7] After reading this, students can be asked to think, write about, and/or discuss how the courses they have taken have helped them to build or strengthen the skills that Cronin describes. Readings might include the many reflections of leaders in the arts and humanities, such as described by Muhlenfeld.[8]

One can continue with an examination of the individual's development of leadership practices. Films such as *Stand and Deliver* or *The Chorus* illustrate ordinary people in the process of "becoming a leader."[9] What is also very important about the films listed above is that students learn about leaders from very different backgrounds, thus providing the diversity that Laird described above. Students can be asked to prepare written analyses of the films, with a focus on how the individual had to change to become a leader. This could involve looking at concepts that may seem like opposites, but when used together can be very powerful.

As leadership generally involves change, it is also very important for students to learn about the nature of change and the influences that result in change—especially influences that go beyond the individual. For example, the film *Lincoln*[10] illustrates how Lincoln himself changed, how he used past ideas to provide support for the abolition of slavery (the Constitution of the United States), and his understanding of what Drucker calls social ecology,[11] namely understanding that the Civil War outcome was now favoring the Union, and that citizens' views about slavery were also changing.

Being Open to Change and Its Processes

Understanding the nature of change and innovation is important for future leaders. Many students think that change and innovation are the result of individual ideas and planning. To counter this view, one could use William Duggan's *Strategic Intuition: The Creative Spark in Human Achievement.*[12] In it are many examples of paradigm shifts and innovations that illustrate leaders who have "borrowed" ideas from the past—whether from science, the arts, business, social enterprise and movements, education, military strategy, and more. What he terms as strategic intuition is about preparing for opportunities, seeing them, and acting on them. Many of the chapters can serve as a short case study that students can analyze. Duggan also reinforces both multidisciplinary thinking and what many disciplines have in common. In Chapter 6, we described how a subject-matter expert develops a module. Duggan's book lends itself to modules such as: Asian religions that use meditation or "presence of mind;" leadership examples from the Civil Rights Movements; and an examination of paradigm shifts in art, music, theatre, and dance. One can also use a film such as *Iron-Jawed Angles*[13] to help students understand the differences between "believe in yourself, set clear goals, and work hard" and "prepare for opportunity, see it, and act on it."[14] While both are tied to self-concept, it is the latter—strategic intuition—that may require more risk, and thus help build a stronger sense of self. Acting on strategic intuition (rather than a plan) also may require a greater sense of autonomy or trust in one's own judgment, again contributing to self-concept.

More advanced students might find Donald A. Schön's *The Reflective Practitioner: How Professionals Think In Action* helpful. In it, he shows how professionals go about solving problems; he argues that they rely less on what they have studied and more on the improvisation they have learned in practice. His concept of "reflection-in-action" adds additional understanding to how leaders are open to new ways of thinking and acting that can lead to creative solutions and innovations that are especially needed in the current world.[15]

Societal Forces

Both of the films *Lincoln* and *Iron-Jaws Angels* illustrate the importance of the societal conditions that can influence the possibilities for and nature of change. Other films include *Glory* and the documentary *No End in*

Sight.[16] The latter is especially suitable for examinations of power/authority, cultural factors, and role/status, which according to Max Weber are central to understanding societies, organizations, and the like. Examining who has power, how is it distributed, and what are the "checks and balances" in making decisions are important questions in this documentary. In particular, students learn to see that leadership is not just about individuals but also societal factors.

The primary goal of providing students with an introduction to leadership is to help them learn to apply concepts from the humanities, sciences, and social sciences in order to better understand the elements of leadership. As noted above, the chapters in Duggan and most of the modules that were developed in our project are drawn from literature, history, philosophy, theatre, religion, music, and art. However, these ideas can also be used in other courses. We turn now to the descriptions of two new courses that were developed to specifically focus, first on the nature of leadership, and second, the importance of ethical leadership.

Theories and Practices of Leadership

This is course (which is an elective for the Business Administration major) focuses on the nature of leadership, primarily at the organizational level. Each of the texts deals with individual, organizational, and societal aspects of leadership. Students learn leadership's inherent connections: individual characteristics, the nature of organizations, and the context of the leadership situation. The course stresses the importance of ethical leadership, and students complete several inventories that help them to better understand their approaches to/practice of leadership. Understanding the practice of ethical leadership enhances students' values about their responsibility to society and others. To take an ethical leadership stand in any setting is to take responsibility, and that is the connection between leadership and societal responsibility. Learning how to take responsibility for ethical actions in leadership positions facilitates the learning of social agency, as described by the scholars of professionalism.[17]

The first set of readings establishes a high goal for the students as future leaders by introducing them to the concept of transforming leadership using the classic *Transforming Leadership* by James MacGregor

Burns,[18] and the highly acclaimed *The Transforming Leader*, edited by Carol S. Pearson.[19] These readings also ground future discussions that occur as students read other leadership texts.

The Individual and Leadership Styles

After they have studied about the global trends and the need for a new kind of leadership, students read *Connective Leadership: Managing in a Changing World* by Jean Lipman-Blumen.[20] Based on theory and empirical research, the "Connective Leadership Model" includes three broad categories of leadership "styles"—direct, relational, and instrumental. Each style contains preferred actions to achieve goals.

Studying these "Achieving Styles" helps students understand that leadership is multifaceted. Most importantly, Lipman-Blumen's book consistently raises issues of ethical leadership and the ethical nature of each of the achieving styles. This is most evident perhaps in her discussion of instrumental approaches, especially what she calls "de-natured Machiavellianism." As students study examples in the text and analyze case studies, the course challenges them to put themselves into similar situations.

The first reading used with the text *Connective Leadership* is from Tricia Turnstell's *Changing Lives.*[21] Students learn about Gustavo Dudamel, *El Sistema*, and YOLA (Youth Orchestra of Los Angeles). As Turnstell writes: "[Dudamel] embodies a compelling idea: that music education can be a means to both individual empowerment and social transformation." (p. xi) The readings tell the story of Dudamel's opening concert at the Hollywood Bowl, at which the parents of YOLA students were given the best seats in the Bowl—at no cost. This gesture to bring families to the Bowl (likely for the first time) strongly affirmed to the entire audience the importance of music's abilities to support social transformation. As our students learn about Dudamel, they identify and describe the achieving styles evident in Dudamel's approach to leadership.

The second case, *Leading Innovation at Kelvingrove*, takes students to a museum in Scotland.[22] It examines the leadership of Mark O'Neill, director of Glasgow Museums, and how he changed the nature and messages of this museum. As the case explains, O'Neill used various approaches to accomplish change. As students examine the behavior of different players via the lens of achieving styles, they become more familiar with a range of leadership styles. And, they may find that an individual uses different styles based on the situation, or on what they have learned in the past—as did O'Neill.

Both cases focus on leaders who have the characteristics of professionals, especially a strong commitment to being a "social-trustee." This point is reinforced in the next set of readings.

Principled and Authentic Leadership

The second book assigned is *The Wizard and the Warrior: Leading with Passion and Power* by Bolman and Deal.[23] Drawing from their earlier work *Reframing Organizations* (see Chapter 6), they focus on the symbolic and political frames. The first chapter gives a quick introduction to the concept of "frames." Students then take the "Leadership Images: A Leadership Self-Inventory," (p. 21) and from this begin to discover which "frame" or "frames" they are most comfortable using and which they tend to avoid.

Chapters in the text examine the natures of the "toxic, relentless, and principled" warriors and of the "authentic, wannabe, and harmful" wizards. They (re) introduce students to different perspectives drawn from sociology, political science, social psychology, and the importance of symbolic meanings. Most importantly, the core of the text makes the distinction between successful ethical leadership, toxic/harmful leadership, and leadership that attempts to be ethical and successful but falls short. Clearly, these ideas lend themselves to extensive discussion of ethical behaviors. Students read and discuss examples, always looking back to their own "frame" preferences.

Faculty also can assign other case studies and ask students to identify the frames evident. Or, students can describe an action or decision they would take justifying their recommendations through the "frame lens." Most importantly, as students analyze the issues in a case, they must provide the ethical support for the recommendations they would make. Examples of cases used with *The Warrior and the Wizard* follow.

The case study *Planned Parenthood Federation of America in 2008* describes some structural (analyst) elements of the organization, raising questions such as: what are the strengths and weaknesses of the structure; should the structure be changed?[24] In the discussion of the case, we ask students to focus on the underlying cultural and symbolic aspects, as well as issues of power. Students are encouraged to recommend changes and discuss the ethical questions such as: what are the ethics of closing PPFA facilities in poor states and the impact that has on the health of women and men. This further opens students' eyes to societal problems and engages them, not as a businessperson or a leader, but as a community and society member.

A second case, *IBM's Decade of Transformation: Uniting Vision and Values* examines the importance of the symbolic and cultural frames, and the need for a "wizard" to move an organization forward (it also gives background for understanding IBM's significant changes described in one of the examples in the Duggan text).[25] Sam Palmisano, a long-time employee, became CEO in 2002. After he inherited a disillusioned workforce and faced significant financial issues, the path he followed focused on IBM's values, involving staff in a "ValuesJam" that invited ideas, criticism, and comments about the future of IBM and its values. This CEO's call to think about company values further enhances students' thinking about a leader's responsibility to others.

From the Individual to Systems Thinking

The final text is *The Necessary Revolution: How Individuals and Organizations Are Working Together to Create a Sustainable World.*[26]. This book uses many of the ideas in *The Fifth Discipline* but also provides short case studies that illustrate how individuals and organizations can collaborate across different boundaries. Because the theme is environmental sustainability, the text addresses a topic that many undergraduate students are passionate about. Therefore, this is an opportune place to make a connection about students' future role in environmental sustainability. Students, as preprofessionals, indeed can practice "social agency" by engaging in environmental issues, modeling what future professionals should in their careers.

Like Bolman and Deal's work, Senge and his colleagues focus on the multiple, and often conflicting, points of view that need to be brought into decision-making. In *The Fifth Discipline,* Senge uses the concepts of "systems thinking, personal mastery, mental models, building shared vision, and team learning." These are also woven into *The Necessary Revolution* via a three-legged stool concept of "core learning capacities for teams:"

- "Understanding complexity" (systems thinking)
- "Aspiration" (personal mastery and shared vision)
- "Reflective conversation" (mental models and dialog)[27]

To explore how these concepts have worked for organizations, the authors provide three chapters that show collaboration across boundaries. Each chapter provides a case study.

- "Never Doubt What One Person and a Small Group of Co-Conspirators Can Do" (an individual begins with his commitment to cleaner-energy cars, shares his vision, and learns from these dialogs = leads to a "Green Zone" in northern Sweden)
- "Aligning an Industry" (building shared vision for greener buildings; many conflicting mental models, years of dialog = results in a LEEDS certification plan for buildings)
- "Unconventional Allies: Coke and WWF [World Wildlife Fund] Partner for Sustainable Water" (these two organizations share knowledge about water resources and its use = leads to better understanding of the need to preserve habitat and community)

From these chapters, students learn about ordinary people from different backgrounds, sometimes with competing interests, who have worked together to make a difference. They see Senge's concepts practiced in real-life situations, which increases their facility to understand and use his ideas. Most importantly, each case shows the elements of professionalism at work. For example, in the first case:

- Per Carstedt used both his expertise about cars and autonomy of judgment when he contacted others to explore ethanol cars for the Swedish market.

- He and his colleagues had strong enough self-concepts to approach owners of filling stations to sell ethanol;
- Collaboration showed recognition of the expertise of others;
- The culmination of the case showed strong elements of social agency, namely building a "Green Zone" that used industrial ecology, drew media attention, and became a model for others to replicate.

The final case study also focuses on environmental issues, providing an example of a well-known firm, whose core business was data, news, and analytics. *Sustainability at Bloomberg, L.P.* traces the evolution of Bloomberg organization's commitment to reduce their carbon footprint through the development of an environmental, social, and governance (ESG) metric, that clients can use to assess the "social responsibility" of a corporation.[28] The case provides examples of organizational change and the use of socially responsible investing, and can be used to explore Senge's concepts.

While students may have heard of Mayor Michael Bloomberg of NYC, they likely think of him as someone with a strong self-concept. However, the case tells them more about his commitment to environmental issues for both the city and the corporation that he founded and bears his name, and about the social agency of Bloomberg and his employees. For example, the main "player" in the case is Curtis Ravenel. An activist with experience on the Recycling Advisory Council, Ravenel served as Bloomberg's Financial Controller for Asia, and was responsible for the BGreen initiative at Bloomberg L.P. His commitments to both environmental and socially responsible investing set the stage for developing and marketing ESG metrics.

While the core of "Theories and Practices of Leadership" is obvious in the title, the course assignments and discussions also deal with the elements of professionalism. For example, as students learn about achieving styles from Lipman-Blumen,[29] they examine impacts on self-concept. As noted above, each of the three books deals with the individual (self-concept), the influences of society through education and other experiences (expertise and autonomy of judgment), and concerns for and contributions to society (social agency). The course stresses the importance of ethical

behavior, and some of the readings and cases encourage students to consider what they would have done in a particular situation.

Humanistic Values and Management

A second course focuses on how the moral dimension of executive leadership affects organizations both internally and externally. It explores how
leadership, which has moral consequences, impacts the achievement of
an organization, its leaders, and its followers. As the foundation course
in ethics, this is where students develop their knowledge of ethical philosophies and different leadership styles, their own leadership style, and
their life mission and purpose. In addition, students learn components of
ethical decision-making including ethical sensitivity, ethical motivation,
ethical judgment, and ethical action.

Many textbooks, with different formats and the contents, could be
used for this course. *Meeting the Ethical Challenges of Leadership: Casting
Light or Shadow* is one example that effectively covers the topics needed
for a foundation course.[30]

We often pair this course with nonbusiness courses such as Documentary Film or Introduction to Globalization. These pairs encourage
students to analyze and learn the ethical process using another discipline,
which, in turn, helps them learn to employ multi-frame thinking. For example, when the course was paired with Documentary Film, the students
learned about the history and evolution of documentary film and how to
analyze films from an ethical perspective. This classroom opportunity to
advance students' ethical processing surely allows them to develop their
professional complexity.

Below is a list of films identified as good candidates for ethical analysis. Via the documentary *The World According to Monsanto*,[31] students
learn how to review and analyze organizational decisions by evaluating
the claims that Monsanto colluded with government, used pressure tactics to have its scientists manipulate scientific data, and used extra-legal
practices—all in order to dominate global agriculture. This documentary
poses questions about how employees, working as managers or scientists
for Monsanto, may have committed unethical acts unknowingly, by
following orders or doing what was expected. Used in conjunction with

Organizational Ethics: A Practical Approach, especially the chapter on "Exercising Ethical Influence," the film opens the door to discussions of the autonomy of judgment, and how business professionals practice it in the workplace.[32]

Another documentary, *Triumph of the Will,* provides a striking example of toxic leadership. It masterfully shows how toxic leaders used threat and fear to control millions of followers, and complements Jean Lipman-Blumen's book *The Allure of Toxic Leadership.*[33] Students learn to recognize different styles of leadership (good, bad, and toxic) and use concepts from history or film to better understand business or vice versa.

Other suggested films include: *The Wonderful, Horrible Life of Leni Riefenstahl,*[34] *Fog of War,*[35] *Harlan County USA,*[36] *Margin Call,*[37] *Why We Fight,*[38] *Why We Fight,*[39] *Frost/Nixon,*[40] *and Amazing Grace.*[41]

It is important to note that this course can be used as a business ethics course within the business major and as a course in the leadership minor.

Integrating Leadership Courses Within the Business Curriculum

The study of leadership, although widespread, has not been formally integrated within the business major. More often, leadership is studied as a separate major at the undergraduate or the graduate level, with some elective courses offered for business students. We believe the plan to allow business students to include leadership courses, as electives within their major, is a valuable approach. Business students naturally gravitate toward leadership studies and value this education within their college years.

Leadership education has been credited with many benefits to students' educations. It has also been a fertile ground for educating business managers. Most managers and scholars accept the basic premise of the "great person" theory of leadership, where it is thought that the study of great leaders is beneficial to one's own heroic side.

It is especially important that students begin to see themselves as leaders. Too often, students cannot compare themselves to one of the great leaders that are often studied in leadership courses—especially women students, as men tend to dominate the list of great leaders. Examples of ethical leadership, drawn from a variety of everyday scenarios that each student can imagine and identify with, have been consciously embedded in our courses via texts, readings, films, case studies, discussions, and assignments.

The call for the rich study of leadership to help in developing professionals is a common and traditional approach. Many business schools see the connection between developing good managers and leadership training, and have added leadership programs to their offerings. Although there are few quantitative studies that link leadership education to an increase in professionalism, it would seem that the association is natural and intuitive. In this chapter, we assembled our approaches in using leadership concepts, either within our business courses, or as separate electives. As noted above, the primary goal is to help students develop a strong, ethical self-concept.

Notes

1. Colby, Ehrlich, Sullivan, and Dolle (2011, p. 47).
2. Laird, Engberg, and Hurtado (2005).
3. Muhlenfeld in Wren, Riggio, and Genovese (2009).
4. Muhlenfeld in Wren, Riggio, and Genovese (2009).
5. Gardner and Laskin (1995).
6. *American Revolutionary: The Evolution of Grace Lee Boggs* (2013).
7. Cronin in Wren, Riggio, and Genovese (2009).
8. Muhlenfeld in Wren, Riggio, and Genovese (2009).
9. *Stand and Deliver* (1988); *The Chorus* (2004).
10. *Lincoln* (2012).
11. Maciariello and Linkletter (2011).
12. Duggan (2013). The version we used is 2007
13. *Iron Jawed Angels* (2004).
14. Duggan (2013). The version we used is 2007
15. Schön (1983); also (1987).
16. *Glory* (1989); *No End in Sight* (2007).
17. Brint (1996); Freidson (2001); Khurana (2007).
18. Burns (2003).
19. Pearson (2012).
20. Lipman-Blumen (2000).

21. Tunstall (2012).

22. Liedtka and Salzman (2009).

23. Bolman and Deal (2006).

24. Grossman, Steenburgh, Mehler, and Oppenheimer (HBSP, 2010).

25. Applegate, Austin, and Collins (HBSP, 2005).

26. Senge, Smith, Kruschwitz, Laur, and Schley (2008).

27. Senge, Smith, Kruschwitz, Laur, and Schley (2008)

28. Marquis, Beunza, Ferraro, and Thomason (HBSP, 2010).

29. Faculty who want to have students learn more about their achieving styles should contact the Connective Leadership Institute to learn about the various inventories.

30. Johnson (2013).

31. *The World According To Monsanto* (2008).

32. Johnson (2016).

33. Lipman-Blumen (2006).

34. *The Wonderful, Horrible Life of Leni Riefenstahl* (1993).

35. *Fog of War* (2003).

36. *Harlan County USA* (1976).

37. *Margin Call* (2011).

38. *Why We Fight* (1942).

39. *Why We Fight* (2005).

40. *Frost/Nixon* (2008).

41. *Amazing Grace* (2006).

CHAPTER 8

Civic Engagement

A Path for Social Agency

Education for democratic citizenship involves human capacities relating to judgment, to choice, and above all, to action. To be literate as a citizen requires more than knowledge and information; it includes the exercise of personal responsibility, active participation, and personal commitment to a set of values.

—Richard L. Morrill[1]

Keywords

Business education, higher education, civic engagement initiatives, benefits of civic engagement, leadership practicum, service-learning, self-concept, social agency

Introduction

Scholars from many fields have called on higher education to strengthen and act upon commitments to prepare graduates for responsible citizenship. In the past few decades, higher education experts and critics have joined the cause, urging colleges and universities to take the lead in encouraging students to address our global society's increasing problems. Notably the mission of liberal learning has included civic engagement for students' growth, maturity, and experience in society.[2] Yet, many academic institutions have had to balance their liberal learning mission with market needs. As noted earlier, scholars have explained that traditionally, academic institutions had high aims and aspirations for institutional missions. However, when federal and state funding decreased, they restructured their programs to depend on other sources of funding, such as private and industry funds.[3] This construct of academic capitalism, as noted by Slaughter and Rhoades, was built on the premise that administrators of educational institutions slowly separated their enterprises from state and federal governments and became closer and more connected to the market.[4]

For the business field, this meant business education had to reinvent itself to become a new capitalistic profession, with an eye toward exploiting the markets rather than training students to uphold a code of ethics for the profession. The growth of industry following World War II created a burgeoning demand for new business professionals. Thus, business education had to balance between teaching for professionalism and teaching for market needs.[5] And when college graduates began to earn high wages for business expertise, "expert knowledge," this indirectly reduced the emphasis on the "social-trustee" facets of professionalism.[6] With these changes, academic institutions began to drift away from their civic missions to educate for democracy and knowledge of civic engagement. This shift has created much tension, with calls from higher education scholars to adhere to the original calling of education. In addition, news of business scandals increased pressure on business programs to emphasize ethics and liberal learning within their programs. The focus is on educating students about civic engagement and what it means to be social-trustees of society.

Definition and Purpose Within Institutions

Civic engagement is defined as the heightened sense of responsibility to community and society in response to a calling. This includes developing civic sensitivity, benefiting the common good, participating in building a civil society, and understanding global citizenship and interdependence.[7] To do so generally involves: developing an informed sense and perspective on social issues of others, self, and the environment; valuing diversity and associations across difference; developing empathy, values, and a sense of social responsibility; assuming leadership and membership roles in organizations; and behaving and working through controversy with civility.[8]

It is important for academic institutions and their programs to choose objectives and approaches that best suit their unique missions. For business schools, the mission of helping their students learn about and practice civic engagement has not been a priority. Rather, the highest priority has been teaching business expertise in the various areas of accounting, finance, management, marketing, and other subjects.[9] As noted earlier, this also may explain the low scores business graduates have relative to social agency, even before the start of their careers.[10] In fact, many managers have been immersed in their business careers, prior to developing an informed sense of societal and global issues.[11] Therefore, it is not a surprise that business managers acting in the field and making decisions that profoundly influence society do not embody the above definitions of engaged citizens.[12]

The perspective that business professionals only need business acumen to conduct business is clearly challenged by the disastrous results of financial scandals locally and globally that proves otherwise. Had these professionals been connected to their communities and trained to serve and engage in society, would they have been as likely to make financial decisions that result in harm to society and its people? While many studies show a positive correlation between college attendance and civic engagement, there is room for improvement. And there is also an urgency, as the studies also show that these business students are not the most engaged among all young people, and engagement of graduates in prior years exceeds those of the more recent ones.[13]

Major Civic Engagement Initiatives in Higher Education

One of the earliest efforts to educate college students in civic engagement is Campus Compact. This organization was founded in 1985 by a group of academic institutions including Brown, Georgetown, and Stanford. Their mission has been to advance public purposes by educating students on civic and social responsibility. In 2006, Campus Compact published two volumes that focus on developing leaders and mobilizing them to lead change while enhancing academic learning: *A Students Guide to Positive Social Change* and *Students as Colleagues: Expanding the Circle of Service Learning Leadership.*[14] The resulting network of state compacts currently totals thirty-four, and provides support for member institutions at the local, state, and regional levels. The state compacts have been instrumental in leading national effort and practices through colloquiums, development of educational materials, and providing professional development to administrators and faculties.

Another important example of organizations with missions to increase civic engagement within educational institutions is the Association of American Colleges and Universities (AAC&U). It advocates for and provides information to both its individual and institutional members. At the center of this organization is the appreciation of diversity, liberal education, and civic engagement. AAC&U advocates a philosophy that cultivates cultural responsibility and liberates the mind. These became the core for their research and recommendations in *College Learning for the New Global Century: knowledge of human cultures and the physical and natural world, intellectual and practical skills, personal and social responsibility, and integrative learning.*[15] The report described the learning and skills that nourish personal and social responsibility. These include: intercultural knowledge and skills for lifelong learning and civic knowledge, both local and global, for educational and professional growth.[16] Another of their publications, which was intended for faculty in all disciplines, is *Toolkit for Teaching in a Democratic Academy.*[17] The toolkit enables students to gain civic skills by participating actively in the classroom community.

There are many other examples of associations similar to Campus Compact and AAC&U. Some support community colleges, and others support disciplinary associations. All of the prior examples signify the importance higher education has placed on the teaching of civic engagement during the college years.

Tangible Benefits of Civic Engagement in College Students

Scholars have outlined definitive outcomes of civic engagement as listed below.[18] In this next section, we will briefly describe each outcome and explain how it might help business students to become business professionals in the future. These benefits accrue to students of all majors; however, based on what we know about business students today, they seem to have a higher need.

Outcome for Learning About the Self

This outcome relates to understanding of oneself in relation to others. This understanding covers identity, social location, historic time, and community.

Self-understanding also relates to the ability to express oneself using his or her own voice to effect change relative to concerning issues.

Self-understanding is important and critical for a business professional trying to conduct business in a local or global community. For instance, a marketing professional who understands the cultural landscape of a targeted market would be more successful than one who lacks it. Another example– a marketing professional who has also been engaged with a local community would be hard-pressed to market a product that has hidden disadvantages or is not beneficial to the targeted buyers. Having a good understanding of the self and the community helps the marketer be more effective in expressing concerns to superiors or co-workers about the product.

Outcome for Civic Learning About Communities and Cultures

This outcome builds one's appreciation of the accumulated wisdom of cultures and communities and enables students to move comfortably from one cultural zone to another, transcending boundaries that divide.

This cultural understanding can be tremendously helpful to a business professional, especially for a global executive trying to manage international divisions; knowledge of personnel issues, especially relative to cultural norms, is necessary to resolve conflicts and create a sense of loyalty to an international parent company. But, also imagine an executive who understands the cultural tradition of a community, but chooses to ignore these traditions, would find him or herself in difficulty. Clearly, the bridge of cultural understanding and awareness results in a more professional behavior and mannerism.

Outcome for Civic Learning About Knowledge

This outcome builds one's understanding that knowledge is dynamic, socially constructed, and can lead to power. Importantly, civic learning allows individuals to link community engagement with democracy. For a business professional, this could be a breakthrough to understand the dynamics of knowledge in society. This can also provide a business professional an appreciation for building democratic and stable power structures in organizations. This political knowledge can also strengthen professional's understanding of business climates and economic cycles.

Outcome for Civic Learning About Skills

Participation in this type of civic learning sharpens students' critical thinking, conflict resolution, and team cooperation. This type of learning relates directly to developing a professional's self-concept via good listening, speaking, and deliberation skills.

For business students who are preprofessionals, these could be gained by serving in nonprofit organizations. Practicing their business skills, being part of a "real" team, taking instructions, meeting deadlines, and presenting their work to colleagues in the organization are all essential skills. Students also experience the nonprofit world in a special setting, with co-workers who are committed to their communities.

Outcome for Civic Learning About Values

This outcome is at the core of civic engagement and it is where students who work in the community on societal causes may face conflicts between their personal and societal values. Imagine a student who is uncomfortable with homosexuality volunteering at an Aids Clinic, or a student who is a conservative Christian working at a Teenage Pregnancy Center. This is the place where students learn to reflect and try to reconcile their social values with those of the external communities around them. It is through these experiences that students develop qualities of character, integrity, empathy, and optimism.

For a business professional, these types of skills make a better manager at any level. A manager who needs to be a role model for employees must have character that is built on empathy and integrity. Through the type of civic engagement described above, business students build tolerance skills, which are a necessary element of building diverse teams. Also beneficial are patience and endurance that one learns as a volunteer in settings that address difficult societal issues.

Outcome for Civic Learning About Public Action

This outcome is based on the constructive participation in communities where one lives and works. Students may join advocacy groups for various causes in order to achieve the end goal for the public good. Students here develop moral and political courage and may work on raising awareness of ethical issues. They may have to take personal risks in order to develop community consciousness of the conflicts they watch. They also have to reconcile their beliefs relative to conflicts they observe.

For future business professionals, this engagement builds strength of character, which they need to navigate in the business world, where a balance between personal goals, company goals, and community's needs has to be achieved. It is through these types of experiences that students learn proper self-expression, while maintaining team-building skills, reporting-to-management skills, and conflict resolution tactics. Additionally, students learn how to advance their causes through a maze of different opinions, beliefs, and goals—no different from a business exercise, working through the different tiers of a multinational company.

The above benefits as outlined by the scholars Jacoby and Musil et al. reflect the current thinking of the higher education community regarding civic engagement.

Maximizing the Educational Capital for Business Students

Presently, these powerful educational reforms suggested above are in early stages of implementation in different programs. Most course-work in business administration programs is still heavily technical with an emphasis on the development of specific expertise—whether it is accounting, marketing, decision sciences, or real estate. Exposure to civic engagement is done at the discretion and interest of the professor. There is more exposure to civic engagement in leadership programs as an experiential component. Perhaps the most hopeful is the recent interest in "diversity literacy" which has dictated the same learning objectives as civic engagement; so many programs have started to offer a diversity component in their civic and global learning education.

At our liberal arts college, up until a decade ago, we offered only few opportunities that facilitated education in the areas of self, community, intercultural understanding, or advancing the public good as described above. We relied on the assumption that students will pick up this knowledge from other liberal arts courses or business offerings at the option of the instructor. However, during our assessment process and student retention efforts, we added one component to our business administration curriculum, a Leadership Practicum class, and enhanced our internship class. The internship class is a 3-credit class and requires the students to have secured employment at either a for-profit or nonprofit organization. The business department deeply believes that students should start their experience in business as soon as possible, and preferably have one or two internships prior to graduation. In addition to gaining experience, this also helps students as they select a sub-discipline in business such as marketing or international business.

The Leadership Practicum component was established as a retention tool for business students in the program. The initial concept was to connect students with each other informally and have nonacademic activities. Wanting to provide a more academic experience, but not add requirement to a large program (51-credits for the major), the new course was offered as an elective for one unit. Students can repeat it multiple times, but receive only a maximum of two units toward the major. Faculty members teaching the course commit only to guide the class, as the actual leadership comes from the students. Admittedly, the program's success often depended on the faculty leading it, and often we had high enrollment in some classes, but not in others. At the beginning of the year, the class started with leadership officers selected from the prior year. These students chose to continue serving from one year to another, since they valued the leadership experience and enjoyed the prestige that the position gave them. Faculty within the department rotated in teaching the class, so they were all familiar with goals of the program and the learning outcomes. Following is a selected list of projects that were sponsored in the program over the years. We will explain some of the student-outcomes that were related to these projects in the next section. Students engaged in the following:

- Sponsored a financial literacy programs in nearby high schools where teams of students prepared and presented a financial lesson in business to other students in high school.

- Served as financial consultants, building business plans for nonprofit organizations
- Built websites and social media sites for nonprofit organizations
- Served as outside directors for a little league team and provided business advice on fund raising and other support projects
- Helped in the local Rotary Club and assisted in various projects and contributed to the establishment of Rotaract (Student-Rotary Chapter)
- Established a fund-raising website and an information center to help citizens in Uganda in their water-pollution problem
- Taught financial management lessons to college students related to debt and credit card management
- Established a SIFE (Students in Free Enterprise) Chapter
- Researched the "Causes of the 2008 Financial Crisis" and presented their findings at several local libraries and Rotary Clubs
- Organized Green-Day events to raise awareness on environmental issues
- Connected with the Lion's Club and assisted in their events
- Organized food-drives to be donated to various nonprofit organizations
- Mentored high-school students who are planning on applying to colleges

At the beginning of the Leadership Practicum program, faculty members had to rely on their own network in the community to establish contact with the Rotary Club, nonprofit organizations, and other community partners. But once the network was established, students were able to continue the communication and pass it on to other students from year to year. One helpful organization was SIFE, which was later renamed as Enactus. This is an organization that is established with the following mission: "A community of student, academic and business leaders committed to using the power of entrepreneurial action to transform lives and shape a better and more sustainable world."[19] Enactus provided broad guidelines with project categories that have been instrumental in helping students design projects and generate ideas. The categories have included the following themes: sustainability, entrepreneurship, and the creation of economic opportunity and financial literacy. Enactus held local and national competitions with member-universities. Sponsoring companies nominated their staff to judge the competitions and select winning teams, thus motivating students to participate in them. However, in recent years, Enactus has held only a national competition, which became prohibitive for our students. However, students have continued to create projects and serve in the community receiving college credits, while expanding their professionalism skills.

In addition to our business program on community engagement, our college participates in a campus-wide effort to engage students in their community. The Community Engagement Center (CEC) has been privately funded by local foundations and by Whittier College for years. Building on our Quaker heritage and its tradition of service, the Center promotes lifelong learning and civic engagement for all disciplines taught, based on the belief that the well-being of the individual is tied to strong communities.

Civic Engagement Development Within Business Courses

As was mentioned earlier, civic engagement encourages students to act upon their elevated sense of responsibility to one's community. Beyond developing civic sensitivity, they can engage in multiple ways, including increased participation in the community and learning to build a civil society that benefits the common good.[20] Business faculty can outline these goals and help students accomplish them in existing business courses. Whittier College has taken it a step further. Students can enroll in the course "Doing Business in China," which was offered as a three-week business elective that involved travel to China. They visited multiple companies, various cultural sites, two environmental agencies, and one major port.

Three texts and one seminal article were used in the course, in addition to multiple case studies and research articles. They are: *Civilization: The West and the Rest* by Niall Ferguson, *Operation China: From Strategy to Execution* by Jimmy Hexter and Jonathan Woetzel, *Factory Girls* by Leslie Chang, and *Understanding China's Urban Pollution Dynamics* by Zheng et al.[21]

The students began with an historical overview of Chinese civilization and began to put in context the reasons for the rise of the West and its dominating power in the world. Most importantly, Ferguson's text provides students a historical foundation on Eastern cultures, but also encourages them to reexamine their views concerning the continuing domination of the West. The text *Operation China* gave them an overview of urbanization and the expansion of business and their social and economic influence on all the regions China. This provided students with a theoretical background on business and economics, which they used in their visits to local and multinational companies in Beijing, Shanghai, and Guangzhou. Students were amazed to see the burgeoning business development of China and we had several discussions revealing the stereotypes they had, as compared to the reality they observed. We visited several large factories, where over 20,000 employees resided in the factory. Students then read the novel *Factory Girls*, which described the lives of migrant works who were part of the largest migration in history of over 130-million migrant workers. The story was told through the lives of two young women who worked in factories similar to the ones the students visited. The novel told the story of how migrant workers leave their homes, farms, and families and migrate to the city to live in crowded-rooms in large apartment buildings. These employees work in factories operating machinery for long hours, having little free time, and often spent in loneliness or with other workers whom they hardly know. And because they may change jobs multiple times during the year, or migrate back to their villages, the dynamics of the workplace keep constantly changing.

These readings combined with the fieldtrips help students to build a broader, more accurate picture of economic growth and its consequences. Students begin to understand that economic growth, higher GDP, and increased wages come at a social price. Discussions and students papers reveal higher levels of understanding of the influence of business on society. They both read about and experience how business decisions lead to unintended consequences and to changes in community structures— such as the lives of migrant workers. This type of class increases students' engagement as citizens in society and in the global community.

Other visits scheduled for the class were to environmental nonprofit organizations in Beijing and Hong Kong. These visits were combined with reading the article "Understanding China's Urban Pollution Dynamics," which explained the status of pollution in China and what is being done about it. The readings also summarized the efforts of government and local agencies to combat the continuing escalation of pollution. We asked the students to summarize the reading and discuss it with each other, prior to the visits to the agencies. The students identified possible questions to ask during the visits and completed the visits with a better understanding of the interworking among business, government and the nonprofit sector. Students observed how community action could produce beneficial change to the society. Students' understanding of the interaction between business, government and nonprofit agencies, and individual community members empowers students to participate and effect change in their own communities.

Observed Outcomes in Participating Business Students

This section offers descriptions of observed learning outcomes of students, while participating in some of the civic engagement initiatives. Although the examples represent a small sample, they provide a glimpse of the expected results that students experience, once they join such a program.

Maturity and Self-discovery

Students selected the projects they wanted to engage in early in the semester. They spent much time exploring the activities offered relative to their skill sets. As this is an important self-discovery task, it is important not to impose activities on students in order to get them to commit to their selection. We asked them to submit a proposal along with expected goals for the project. Although the students were generally overly optimistic about reaching their goals for the semester, it is important that faculty reserve judgment and provide positive feedback at this point. For example, one of our recurring projects is to teach high schools students about finances. Students were supposed to contact high schools, explain the goal of the projects, schedule dates, prepare lesson plans, and collect feedback from high-school students. Because some students waited too long to contact high schools, their initial number of planned presentations dropped significantly. They also underestimated the amount of preparation needed for a lesson plan and they reported, at times, that they were unprepared for questions. Students had to coordinate with other team members participating in the activity and frequently they had disappointments along the way. They also had to coordinate practice sessions, prior to the actual event to work on their presentations. On the date of the event, they had to dress professionally, schedule shared rides, arrive on time, and convince teachers and students in the classroom of their professional skills. At the end, students reported positive interactions with high-school students and feeling of confidence, being the teacher in the classroom. The entire experience developed students' maturity in terms of setting goals, leading teams, and coordinating with community members.

Improved Self-concept

Students who participated in the Leadership Practicum Course joined the class to obtain additional credits, have a leadership experience, and/or wanted to join a business group to forge a closer connection to the major. The first two weeks focused on the intended goals, how the students were supposed to integrate themselves in a community project, and the reasons and importance of doing so. One of the primary activities for students was to engage in local Rotary Club activities. Rotary members were supportive of students' participation and invited them to their weekly meetings. At students' requests, Rotary members attended students' weekly planning meetings and provided feedback on students' plans, generated ideas, brainstormed projects, and provided real-life experience—especially since these Rotarians were often former or present executives at local companies or retired professionals in the community.

An example of this collaboration involved a Rotary member who asked one of our teams to explore the reasons and remedies for the 2008 financial crisis and to present it to several Rotary chapters. Students were intrigued by this challenge and excited about further engagement with Rotary members. Students started by conducting research, often guided by Rotary members, discussed their materials, and then prepared presentations. Rotary members who were guiding the project served as the audience for students' rehearsals of their presentations. A result was that students reported a tremendous improvement of their own self-concept. Specifically, they felt more confident about engaging with executives, improved their professional mannerisms during the process, and gained lifelong relations with members in the community. Students who participated in at least two semesters or more of the Leadership Practicum Course showed further improvements in leadership, appreciation for community leaders, and enhanced professional skills overall.

Responsibility to the Community

Connecting students to their communities is an important task since it helps students' understanding of communities and cultures, broadens their understanding of business knowledge and puts it in perspective, and enhances civic skills, including critical thinking, communication, and conflict resolution (Jacoby, 2009).[22] However, most business students are strongly encouraged to do business internships, especially to gain experience in business functions. Therefore, it is difficult for business students to reap the benefits of civic engagement as described above, which contributes to uneven commitments to professionalism as mentioned in earlier chapters. The purpose of this chapter is to raise faculty's awareness of opportunities that could be incorporated in business programs without overloading the major with additional credits. Faculty members can incorporate projects within their courses that would increase students' chances to engage in their communities. The previous example of working with Rotary Chapters is an excellent one since it joins business leadership with community engagement.

Additionally, if a business program allows an internship to count as an elective, this requirement can be modified to include experiences at non-profit organizations, further facilitating students' exposure to communities. At Whittier College, we allowed this model. Many of our students worked at nearby nonprofit organizations including Whittier's First-Day (for homeless), The Little League, Intercommunity Counseling Center, Spiritt Family Services, Chamber of Commerce, and many others. Most of the students helped in financial, marketing, and management tasks, but the exposure to the organizations and communities they served gave them a critical nonbusiness dimension. At Intercommunity Counseling

Center (ICC) where the center provided counseling, psychological evaluations and treatment for community members at reduced rates, students helped to put together a business plan. This gave them direct access to top managers and directors in the organization and helped them understand the financial needs of the center, including fund raising and grant writing. They also assisted in the daily tasks of the center, where they were faced with the reality that community members needed help and assistance. The linked assignment of business and community expanded the context of their business knowledge. The business plan they helped developed with estimates of number of patient visits, now translated to faces and personalities. It was interesting to watch students become fully committed to the Center's success and grant writing prospects as they gained understanding of their operation.

In another project, students volunteered their business knowledge assisting at Whittier's First Day. The Center assists homeless citizens to transition to employment and housing. Students reported how they arrived at the center with stereotypes about the center, the homeless citizens, and the neighborhood and community. After a few visits, students reported a reality "shock" with their exposure, revealing incorrect assumptions they have made. Homeless citizens were intelligent, social, and relatable. They came in all sorts of ethnicities, race, color, and socioeconomic backgrounds. They became homeless for many reasons outside of their control. They had hopes and dreams, and they wished to improve their situation. Students learned that they often do so with help and assistance. This experience helped expand students' understanding of community and culture and allowed them to reflect effectively on the diverse cultures around them. Many students communicated that the experience provided meaning to their lives, where they felt rewarded by their experience. Many also reported feeling more obligations to the citizens of the community. Residents at the center reciprocated the learning providing students with their own experiences and sharing their knowledge. In the process, residents began to change their old assumptions about learning, realizing that new learning is still a possibility for them. Although students volunteered at the center to gain business experience, they were able to attain far more than that. This experience, which included written assignments, speaking assignments, and reflections, allowed students to address issues of diversity. These issues crossed cultural boundaries and helped them compare civic and business traditions. A faculty member may supplement students' experience with a theoretical resource that helps students put their experience in context. We suggest the article *Creating Cultural Connections: Navigating Difference; Investigating Power and Unpacking Privilege.*[23]

It is easy to imagine a business student who has been through a program of business classes that teach only knowledge and expertise, and another student where the program engages students in the community, while learning business skills. Not unlike our belief that students' participation in sports assists their sportsmanship and team-participation skills, interaction with the "other" teaches lessons about community engagement. Therefore, it is easy to understand why the higher-education community encourages colleges and universities to include civic engagement in their programs, since these experiences have such an influence on students' education and their growth toward professionalism.

Notes

1. Morrill (1982).
2. Jacoby and Associates (2009).
3. Slaughter and Rhoades (2004).
4. Slaughter and Rhoades (2004).
5. Brint (1996); Colby, Ehrlich, Sullivan, and Dolle (2011).
6. Brint (1996).
7. Coalition for Civic Engagement and Leadership (2007).
8. Coalition for Civic Engagement and Leadership (2007).
9. Khurana (2007); Nino (2014).
10. Colby, Ehrlich, Sullivan, and Dolle (2011); Nino (2014).
11. Khurana (2007); Swanson (2009).
12. Nino (2014); Swanson (2009).
13. Lopez, Kirby, Sagoff, and Herbst (2005); Kiesa, Orlowski, Levine, Both, Kirby, Lopez, and Marcelo (2007).
14. Cone, Kiesa, and Longo (2006); Zlotkowski, Longo, and Williams (2006).
15. Musil (2005).

16. National Leadership Council for Liberal Educations and America's Promise (2007).
17. Meade and Weaver (2004).
18. Musil (2006).
19. http://enactus.org/who-we-are/our-story/
20. Jacoby and Associates (2009); Musil (2006).
21. Ferguson (2011); Hexter and Woetzel (2013); Chang (2009); Zheng and Kahn (2013).
22. Jacoby and Associates (2009).
23. Reitenauer, Cress, and Bennett (2005).

CHAPTER 9

Conclusions and the Path Forward

The walls around many business schools remain high, eroding interdisciplinary education and research collaboration that might address some grand challenges facing society. In response, we . . . argue business schools should lower their walls to engage with other academic departments to address such grand challenges in a way that engenders social value.

—Currie, et al.[1]

Keywords

Business education, higher education, change agents, liberal learning, professional programs, autonomy, social agency, self-concept

Introduction

This book has been about lowering the walls at Whittier College, but its lessons can be applied to other institutions. We were fortunate to have generous funding from the Andrew W. Mellon Foundation, and it was primarily the faculty in Business Administration and Humanities who embraced the idea and did most of the labor. Our work is ongoing as we continue revisions to courses, explore new ideas, and apply our ideas to other professional programs (again with Mellon support). Our goals are to continue to push toward a new definition and type of professional curricula. With this ideal in mind, this chapter will provide some recommendations about getting there; however, we begin with our stories of how we became involved.

Lana Nino took a traditional path toward a profession, graduating from college with a Bachelor's Degree in accounting. She joined Arthur Andersen & Co. and later became a Certified Public Accountant. To qualify, she had to take a series of tests that included an ethics exam. During her climb up the corporate ladder—in multiple positions as controller, director of internal audit, and chief financial officer—she experienced multiple challenges where she needed to have moral courage. She found that her biggest challenges in the work place were to practice multi-framing of situations and autonomy, none of which she had learned in her courses in business and accounting. Her next journey was to join academia, teaching at a liberal arts college. She soon also returned to the university to earn her doctorate in Higher Education at the University of California, Riverside. As described in an earlier chapter, she focused on business education as her topic for her dissertation. It was then that she began to realize the deficiencies in her own education, which influenced her career experiences in business. Even though she was educated as a professional, she felt she lacked many of the professional skills that she now thought she was supposed to pick up during her many years in undergraduate and MBA programs. She also recalled many other professionals she had encountered and worked with, including CFOs, controllers, and vice presidents in business, who fit the description in the literature of professionals who focused on expertise and lacked social agency. It was then that she decided to dig deeply into the literature on "professionalism" and the intended higher education path for professionals. Teaching at a liberal arts college and going to conferences steeped in that type of education (such as the Wye Faculty Seminar and several AAC&U conferences), she began to see the benefits of bringing the liberal arts into the classroom. More importantly, she began to see the urgency of educating business students as preprofessionals; always keeping in mind the professionals she dreamed they would become, and how much of a difference they would make in society. As a faculty member, she modified her teaching of accounting to empower students to think of the accounting curriculum with an eye toward professionalism. She asked students their thoughts on how the rules and regulations were constructed and how they can participate as future professionals in continuing that effort. As a department chair, she stressed the importance of integrating other disciplines within business courses resulting in new paired-courses and modules within business content. She also stressed the importance of connecting students with their community, implementing many programs for students to engage through internships and leadership programs.

Susan Gotsch took a different route to learn about professionalism, ethics, and business. After her undergraduate degree in history, she earned a Master's Degree in political science. Her Ph.D. in sociology was steeped in theory, in particular that of Karl Marx, Max Weber, Emile Durkheim, and Erving Goffman. This is what she taught for a decade. When she was encouraged to become an academic dean, she read Bolman and Deal's *Reframing Organizations* and found parallels to these theorists, whose works guided her through twenty years as academic dean. During her time at three small liberal arts colleges, she worked closely with faculty on curriculum, including the Humanities in Management Institute at Hartwick College. From these experiences, she knew that collaboration across disciplines was not only possible, but also fun and valued. When she joined the faculty ranks at Whittier College, she was invited to teach "Management and Organizational Behavior." Exposure to the plethora of case studies and management scenarios pushed her to ask questions about ethics and management. Jeff Decker and Lana Nino (both in Business Administration) provided excellent guidance and learning. And as fate would have it, the Mellon Foundation was interested in the intersections of business and the humanities.

As we began our journey together, we were especially guided by two important studies. The first was the in-depth research and recommendations made in *Rethinking Undergraduate Business Education: Liberal Learning for the Profession.*[2] The second was Nino's work that examined differences in certain elements of professionalism, comparing undergraduate business majors and students in other majors. Both pointed toward the need for change and both focused on the importance of the concept of "business as a profession" as an essential element of change. Colby and her colleagues provided strong recommendations about the business curriculum, which we have paraphrased to fit our institution: strong liberal education as part of the requirements; incorporation of "liberal learning" into the curriculum, focusing on intentional linkages; collaboration between business educators and faculty in the liberal arts that result in learning for all.[3] We hope that our discussions about and examples of the curricular changes in Whittier College's business administration major illustrate that it is possible to address these recommendations. But it has also been Nino's research and guidance about "undergraduates as prepro-fessionals" that helped us drill down into what this means and how we can foster it. But how does one get started with change?

Being a Change Agent

Rosabeth Moss Kanter's article "Leadership for Change: Enduring Skills for Change Masters" provides excellent advice about the stages of change.[4] They begin with having the ability to be—in Drucker's words—a social ecologist who can sense and deal with both dangers and opportunities. Being open to new ideas, and perhaps creating them, is important. Leaders of such efforts as curricular change need to be able to communicate a vision, and more importantly, engage others in spreading the ideas. Engaging others can develop into coalitions, which means that political strategies are important. Periodic "nurturing"—of those who are working toward change—is essential. And then there are often the "difficult middles [that] require persisting and persevering."[5] (p. 11) And finally, there is the need for people to be recognized publicly for their work. For us, there were bumps along the way, but we learned much from Kanter.

Advice About Change

To begin the process of change, we followed some suggested actions of Colby and her colleagues (Pp. 171–176). But we were also guided by recommendations for change agents written decades ago in *Educating Professionals: Responding to New Expectations for Competence and Accountability.* In the chapter "Priorities of Change in Professional Education" the authors list key principles that change agents should understand, as follows:

- Change is political, and thus not necessarily logical, and thus requires political strategies.
- Change is incremental and adaptive, not immediate and precipitous.

- . . . Change moves successively through several layers of support, thus making it imperative that "innovators" and "early adopters" be identified early and supported.
- Planning and implementation of change require participation by those most affected by it.
- Change requires persistence and flexibility from those who champion it."[6] (p. 326)

Needless to say, our goals and tasks seemed overwhelming. So we want to provide some advice and raise questions to think about, before you begin a similar journey. The following observations are meant to help colleagues on other campuses begin the conversations about professionalism and the business major. Curry and Wergin stated in their Preface for *Educating Professionals* that: "regardless of where the pressures for change originate, real change begins with the professional school faculty and its leadership." (p. xiii) This certainly was our experience, as our beginnings were with business faculty and the College's President. Thus we note that our recommendations may be more pertinent for deans or faculty or both, so we combine them as a way of encouraging this kind of collaboration.

In becoming change agents, it is not uncommon for faculty or academic deans who are attempting to change curriculum to focus—borrowing from Bolman and Deal—on the structural, political, and human resources aspect of change. Forgotten are the cultural and symbolic elements, which are usually deeply imbedded, often harder to change, and often seen as the "soft" elements of change. So we begin with the advice that change agents should thoroughly understand the culture of the departments that will be involved or impacted, to be aware of the student culture(s) of these departments, to be familiar with the leadership and culture of faculty committees that will be involved, and to consider the overall culture of the institution. A second symbolic issue is whether there are faculty and administrative leaders who believe in the need to "humanize" business education. And are there faculty members, especially in the humanities, who could and would collaborate with business administration faculty? Are there "players" who understand the importance of institutional culture? This is not to say that the structural, political, and human resource frames are not important for change agents. But research in many fields—anthropology, literature, psychology, political science, religious studies, sociology, theatre—point to the importance of symbols and their cultural meanings.

Yet it is also essential to understand the political/power elements of change. As Curry and Wergin note: "professional schools are *political systems* . . . with a *culture that inhibits change.*"[7] (p. 322) Needless to say, support from high-level administrators is essential, especially if you plan to seek external funding for your project. What does the Vice President for Academic Affairs think about integrating liberal arts into the business major? Are there other departments that might be engaged to help? Are there faculty members who are willing to lead the project? If the answers to these questions are encouraging, engage the most interested faculty in getting started.

Getting Started

Finding common interests with a colleague you respect is essential for getting started. It requires the good will of several players—in Senge's terms—to engage in dialogue and find common ground. Two examples of modules illustrate this: Nino and McEnaney (history) were interested in ethical leadership; and Gotsch and Kjellberg (Philosophy) were interested in eastern philosophies. The results were not only modules (see Chapter 6), but also continued visits to each other's classes. To the extent that institutions have faculty development funds, the dean could provide some time or financial incentives to encourage these activities. And if interdisciplinary learning is important, then department members and deans can evaluate a candidate's commitment to such in the hiring and tenure processes.

Once ideas start percolating, it is also important to pilot some of the activities that are generated. It will be easy to find faculty in the humanities who strongly feel that business students should study ethics. Encouraging them to participate in some way is a good next step: asking them to work with business faculty to find case studies that have an ethical dimension, to be used, for example, in a marketing class. Other faculty may be immersed in service learning, and could thus exchange ideas with business faculty. Curriculum committees could be invited into discussion about interdisciplinary learning. Involve colleagues in discussions based on such readings as Khurana, Trank and Rynes, and Currie et al., which call for the increase of professionalism and interdisciplinary learning in business.[8]

Keeping Up the Momentum

It is common that during some phase of change, it is hard to keep going. There are lots of "difficult middles." At these times, it would be wise to take stock and focus on which collaborations are likely to be successful and have the most impact. Also, encourage faculty to pilot an idea, module, or revised course. Begin to discuss the successes, but also examine possible revisions for the less successful. Ask students what they experienced in the changed business courses. And faculty in the liberal arts can be strong advocates for change—by encouraging others to work with business faculty to develop modules or develop a linked course. At each stage, you will want to have clear goals, faculty engagement, and some support for faculty development, so that you are able to encourage and lead others when momentum slows.

We would also agree with Sharon Daloz Parks, who urges leaders to use the metaphors of the arts, which she sees as "mere stepping-stones to a yet more significant shift—the transformation of the prevailing myth of leadership from hero to artist."[9] (p. 1) Her metaphors are good advice to those leaders who face the common challenges of "affirmation and resistance . . . working on the edge . . . interdependence with the medium . . . and improvisation." (Pp. 9–13) We easily see these challenges in theatre, music, and art, but seldom look for them in leadership. Jazz has much to teach leaders: having a structure, but one that requires direction, listening to others, being intuitive about new possibilities, and innovation—or as Parks states:

> Whether adaptive leadership is practiced in the corporation, the neighborhood, or within an international alliance, it does, indeed, require something very much like the artistry of skilled jazz musician—bringing tradition, intuition, technique, and the power of imagination and innovation to that edge where the toughest challenges and greatest possibilities are located.[10] (Pp.13–14)

The changes that we made to the Business Administration curricula have been rewarding for faculty and students, and we will continue with the momentum. We believe that we are on the right track, as evidenced by various assessments we have done.

Assessment of the Results

Early in the project, several faculty and staff were fortunate to attend the "2012 Summer Institute on Integrative Learning and the Departments" that was sponsored by the Association of American Colleges and Universities (AAC&U). Central to our work were intensive workshops on collaboration, integrative work on majors, and most importantly, developing assessment tools with which to examine our results. During the weeklong Summer Institute, we worked very closely with Jo Beld (Director of Evaluation and Assessment and Professor of Political Science at St. Olaf College). In Spring 2013, we were able to being Beld to campus, and she spent two days working with individuals and groups on ways to assess the outcomes of the changes we were making. These included faculty, the chair of the College's Academic Assessment Committee, colleagues who are responsible for learning outcomes assessment, the Vice President for Student Life and the director of Student Life's leadership programs. Jo Beld returned later in the year and continued to work with faculty on the assessment tools as shown in Table 9.1. Examples of students' results are shown in Figure 9.1.

In the pairs "Humanistic Values in Management" and "Documentary Film Movements and Genres," students were asked to indicate the level of impact that the pairs contributed to these abilities: prepared for ethical leadership, assessing own ethical development, using more than one perspective, resolving ethical dilemmas, and preparing to practice ethical leadership. The percentage of students who answered "High" or "Very High" ranged from 86 percent for "assessing own ethical development" to 100 percent for "using more than one perspective." When asked about how the pairs helped to achieve certain elements of liberal learning, students' perceptions ranged from 85 percent for "understanding other cultures" to 100 percent for "thinking critically." Figure 9.1 below shows the full results.

Table 9.1 Paired-Courses Assessment

Students were asked to answer each question based on the level of impact it had on them. The results are shown in Figure 9.1.

• To what extent did this pair of courses contribute to your abilities in each of the following areas?

Response options: Extensively; Substantially; Somewhat; Very little; Not relevant to this pair

1. Recognizing the ethical demands of the leadership role
2. Recognizing, analyzing, and resolving ethical dilemmas using theoretical frameworks
3. Examining situations from more than one ethical perspective
4. Assessing your own ethical development
5. Preparing to practice ethical leadership yourself by choosing moral behaviors, exercising moral influence, and expressing your own moral values

---

• To what extent did this pair of courses help you make progress in achieving each of the goals of the Whittier Liberal Education program?

Response options: Extensively; Substantially; Somewhat; Very little; Not relevant to the pair

6. Your ability to use ideas and information from more than one field of study to understand and analyze a topic or issue
7. Your ability to communicate effectively in writing
8. Your ability to communicate effectively in listening and speaking
9. Your ability to think critically
10. Your ability to explain how you are connected with others, whether physically, historically, socially, and/or globally
11. Your understanding of one or more cultures in addition to your own
12. Your ability to offer more than one perspective on, or interpretation of, a topic or issue

---

• How important was each of the following elements in helping you connect what you were learning across the two courses?

Response options: Very important; Important; Somewhat important; Not very important

13. Having both instructors attend most class sessions in both courses
14. Hearing each instructor refer to information or ideas from the other course during class
15. Field trips involving both courses
16. The inclusion of information or ideas from both courses in course examinations
17. Course readings that drew on information or ideas from both fields of study represented in the courses
18. Film/documentary analysis

Contributions to Students' Abilities

Prepared for ethical leadership

Assessing own ethical development

Using more than one perspective

Resolving ethical dilemmas

Ethical demands

Legend: Very high, High, Other

0   5   10   15   20

Achieve Goals of Liberal Learning

Offer multiple perspectives

Understanding other cultures

Explain connection to others

Think critically

Listening and speaking skills

Writing skills

Analyze from multiple fields

Legend: Very high, High, Other

0   5   10   15   20   25   30

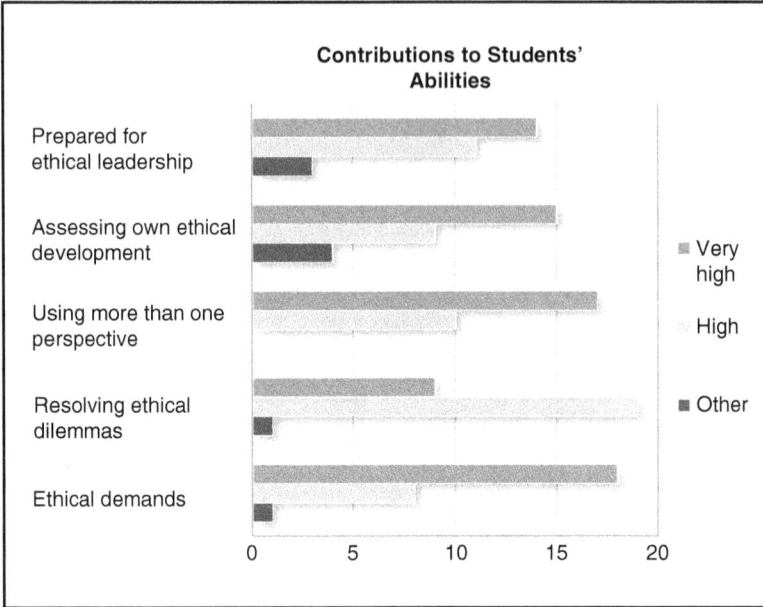

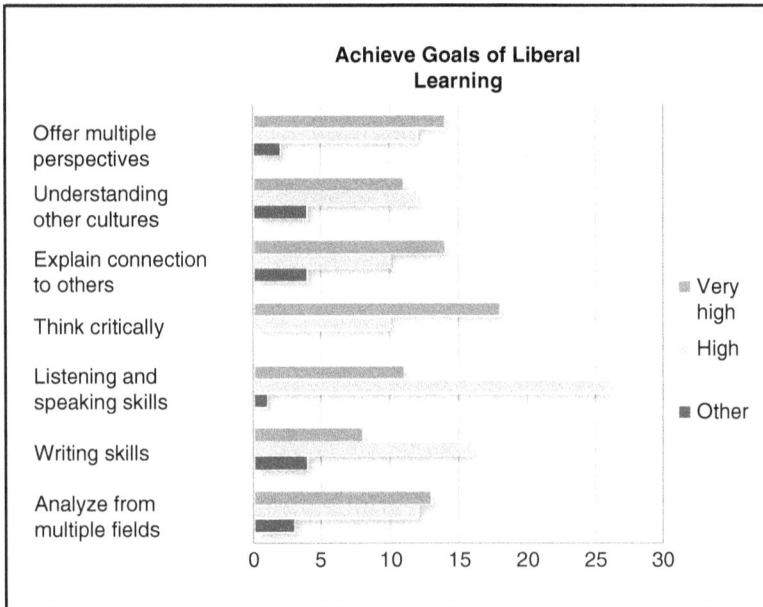

Figure 9.1 Learning Impact Questionnaire Result.

Table 9.2 Module Assessment

1. **To what extent did this module contribute to your abilities in each of the following:**
Extensively; Substantially; Somewhat; Very little; No effect
   1. Recognizing the ethical demands of the leadership role
   2. Examining situations from more than one ethical perspective
   3. Assessing your own ethical development
   4. Preparing to practice ethical leadership yourself by choosing moral behaviors, exercising moral influence, and expressing your own moral values

2. **To what extent did this module help you make progress in achieving each of the goals of the Whittier Liberal Education program?**
Extensively; Substantially; Somewhat; Very little; No effect
   5. Your ability to use ideas and information from more than one field of study to understand and analyze a topic or issue
   6. Your ability to communicate effectively in listening and speaking
   7. Your ability to think critically
   8. Your ability to explain how you are connected with others, whether physically, historically, socially, and/or globally
   9. Your understanding of one or more cultures in addition to your own
   10. Your ability to offer more than one perspective on, or interpretation of, a topic or issue

Faculty also prepared their own assessment tools for modules created in each other's courses. An example of a module assessment is listed in Table 9.2. Similar questionnaires were used for other courses, and results are similar. For example, students in the pair "Sustainable Development and the Triple Bottom Line" and "Soils and Environmental Geomorphology" reported that the pair contributed "very highly" to their abilities about: "ethical decisions, communication with the team, bringing knowledge to the team, and critical thinking."

In addition, students said that the pairs' contribution was very high, especially in helping them: "offer multiple perspectives, understand other cultures, and do analyses from multiple fields."

In closing, we offer recommendations that we consider important, and one's that can help us and hopefully others, to attain the "end product" of the helping undergraduate business students develop all of the aspects of professionalism.

Recommendations

The following provides a succinct description of important elements that we have suggested in earlier chapters, organized by recommendations that call for using professionalism as a platform and presenting practical ways to develop professionals. Importantly, they involve both curricular and cultural elements.

1. **Adopt a curriculum that would assist in the development of the professional. Business has a higher purpose in society other than an entrepreneurial one. Faculty should stress the higher purpose of business in the different sub-disciplines.**

    a. Professionals join their professions due to a calling and they have a stronger connection to their discipline if they can connect with the cause. Preprofessionals develop pride in their selected profession if they know the higher purpose. In Chapter 3, we discussed teaching for the higher purpose of business. In Table 3-2, we showed the difference from teaching expertise to teaching the higher purpose and expertise.

    b. Build your own interdisciplinary courses or work with faculty in other disciplines to do so. Interdisciplinary courses enrich business curriculum and allow students to use multi-frames and different views of issues. Carefully examine if there are a few courses in the liberal arts that should be required for business majors.

    c. Above, we talked about the difference between the current curriculum and a proposed professional curriculum. We propose that business schools specifically target two courses for the development of the individual. One course is the introductory course to business and society and the other course is a foundational

Table 9.3 Professional Focused Curriculum

Business Expert Curriculum	Business Professional Curriculum
• Business and society	• Business, society, and the professional
• Marketing	• Marketing through the lens of professionalism
• Elective in business ethics	• Foundation in business ethics and the professional
• Research papers in courses	• Business research methods course
• Business law	• The ethical, legal, and professional challenges of business managers

business ethics course. In both courses, the curriculum should be modified and written with the future professional in mind. The list in Table 9.3 can be used to guide such change.

2. **Business has a higher purpose in society other than an entrepreneurial one. Faculty should stress the higher purpose of business in the different sub-disciplines.**

   a. As mentioned before professionals join their professions due to a calling. This needs to be reinforced in the curriculum, as described above, as well as in the instruction provided by the faculty teaching the subjects. In Chapter 3, we discussed teaching for the higher purpose of business. In Table 3.2, we showed the difference from teaching expertise to teaching the higher purpose and expertise. We hope that educators can reframe their explanations to serve the higher cause.

3. **Given that the AACSB recommends an approach to integrate ethics into all business subjects, we recommend that business faculty receive proper training on teaching ethics within their subject.**

   a. This can be accomplished by offering continuing education opportunities for business faculty, such as:

      i. Conferences that deal with the liberal arts, for example the annual meeting of the Association of American Colleges and Universities, and/or the joint Phi Beta Kappa/American Conference of Academic Deans conference on the liberal arts

      ii. Participation in the Wye Faculty Seminar, which focuses on the humanities through readings of classical and contemporary works. Lana Nino attended this in (2008) and her experience was crucial to our project

   b. Business faculties, who have had these opportunities, can provide on-campus workshops for their colleagues.

   c. As part of this, business faculty should be encouraged to weave ethical themes into their courses (as recommended by AACSB)—perhaps by using case studies, modules, or team teaching. This may require some faculty development that examines the concepts of ethical sensitivity, ethical judgment, ethical motivation, and ethical action. By focusing their students first on ethical sensitivity and motivation, they invite them to: approach ethical situations by looking deeply into the circumstances; engage in multi-framing and visualization; experience the ability to put oneself into the situation; and understand various societal views on an issue. All these will help strengthen autonomy and social agency in each student.

4. **Require a foundational course in business ethics.**

   a. Critical to a foundation in ethics is a foundational business ethics course, such as that described in Chapter 4. Students need to understand the discipline of ethics before they are ready to deal with ethical questions in their other business courses. One may choose to use business cases, but by using cases from other fields, students see that business ethics cases are not the only examples of ethical failures and gain practice in critiquing actions that are unethical.

5. **Integrate more research and theory within the business curriculum**.

   a. We suggest that a business course such as one about managing organizations can serve as place for students to develop their capacities for interdisciplinary learning, multiple-frame thinking, and understanding how research and theory—beyond economics—are essential in the field of business. Careful selection of texts and case studies can contribute to students' development of professional characteristics (#1 above), especially to strengthen ethical sensitivity and autonomy in business students.

   b. Infuse leadership theories and research in various business classes or electives. Careful selection from the extensive literature on leadership is a good source to help students develop the self-concept they need to become strong, autonomous professionals. Some of this literature provides ways for students to learn more about their own leadership qualities—relative to the literature that describes qualities of good, ethical leaders. Focusing on this can influence students' ideas about self-concept and also assist students to become better business managers and professionals.

   c. Teach theoretical thinking and demand evidence of it in students' assignments.

6. **Provide opportunities for students to practice social agency.**

   a. The importance of social agency can be taught, but it also needs to be experienced. Learning about diversity, other cultures, and the influence of business on society are an important start for understanding social agency. But it is essential to develop applied methodologies that help students to <u>develop</u> social agency. By this we mean getting the student actually to practice social agency. One way is to use the literature that Gentile developed in *Giving Voice to Values*.[11] This innovative curriculum helps students to express their autonomy and voice their values. Their actions in doing so can be built on their professional identity, as molded by the humanities.

   b. Other examples that can increase social agency involve engagement in communities and/or study abroad. The "where" is especially important if it gets the student out of her culture or his safety zone. Examples include service-learning courses, volunteer work in a nonprofit organization (especially if its clients are very different from the student), or study-abroad in areas such as the Middle East, Africa, Asia, or Latin America.

7. **Build spaces for students to practice professional autonomy in the classroom and outside.**

   a. Classroom discussions should always include multi-framing and dialectical approaches to arguments. This helps students develop their voice. Business students especially get little time to do this in the classroom due the density of disciplinary material. If faculty members understand the importance of professional autonomy in students' futures, they will create the time and space for them to practice it.

   b. Provide opportunities for students to present research papers in class, perhaps in lieu of a final examination. Have students create teams and then debate a research topic from opposite views (e.g., defense spending, legalization of marijuana, increase or lower taxes in the U.S.). This is a very helpful exercise since students do more reflection in research.

   c. Encourage students to present their research at peer-reviewed conferences.

8. **Professional programs should function with the spirit of professionalism within their undergraduate and graduate programs.**

   a. Adopt a code of ethics for business schools and departments, and include faculty, staff, and students within its purview. Have students review and discuss the code of ethics in business classes before they sign it.

   b. Have students join professional organizations early in their programs such as the AAA, AMA, or other. Students' awareness of professional organizations allows them to observe professionals and commits them to joining a profession rather than just completing a major in college.

   c. Engage business faculty in social agency. If students are able to observe their faculty serve in the community, they are much more likely to become engaged and develop care for their community and the broader society.

Final Thoughts

Today's relentless economic, technological, and cultural changes require a deeper look at how professional schools build and deliver their programs. Arguably, business education is more important than ever in U.S. higher education due to its significant influence on society. Adopting a professional model for delivering a business program is an urgent societal need, even if it requires more resources. However, many of the changes suggested in this book can be implemented by changing content and instructional approach of business texts. The mere awareness of the need to develop students' autonomy and social agency can make a difference in the classroom. Even with the tide of online learning, a professional approach can still be implemented. Business faculties who begin to think of their students as preprofessionals can always modify their content and assignments to stress elements of professionalism in their online instruction. Deans and department chairs of business programs can monitor success of implementation. Most of our business faculty would welcome a change that would improve business graduates and thus society. Indeed the call for professionalism, although an old framework, is still what is needed today to drive change.

Notes

1. Currie, Davies, and Ferlie (2016).
2. Colby, Ehrlich, Sullivan, and Dolle (2011).
3. Colby, Ehrlich, Sullivan, and Dolle (2011).
4. Kanter (2005). This is the version that we used
5. Kanter (2005).
6. Curry and Wergin (1993).
7. Curry and Wergin (1993).
8. Currie, Davies, and Ferlie (2016); Trank and Rynes (2003).
9. Parks (2005).
10. Parks (2005).
11. Gentile (2010).

References

American Bar Association. (2016). Retrieved October 28, 2016. www.american bar.org

The Association to Advance Collegiate Schools of Business ACSB. (2003). Retrieved June 30, 2010. www.aacsb.net

The Association to Advance Collegiate Schools of Business (AACSB). (2004). *Ethics education in business schools*. Report of the ethics education task force to AACSB International's Board of Directors. Retrieved October 28, 2016. www.aacsb.net

AACSB. (2006). *Eligibility procedures and accreditation standards for business accreditation*. Tampa, FL: Association to advance Collegiate Schools of Business.

Abbott, A. (1988). *The system of professions: an essay on the division of expert labor*. Chicago, IL: University of Chicago Press.

Achbar, M., and J. Abott. "The Corporation." Canada: Zeitgeist Films, 2004.

Adams, D., & Miller, B. K. (2001). Professionalism in nursing behaviors of nurse practitioners. *Journal of Professional Nursing, 17*(4), 203–210.

Adler, N. J. (2015). Finding beauty in a fractured world: art inspires leaders—leaders change the world. *Academy of Management Review, 40*(3), 480–494.

Adler, P. S. (2002). Corporate scandals: it's time for reflection in business schools. *Academy of Management Executive, 16*(3), 148–149.

Applegate, L., Austin, R., & Collins, E. (2005). IBM's decade of transformation: uniting vision and values. Boston, MA: *Harvard Business School Publishing, 9-802-127.*

Apted, Michael. *"Amazing Grace."* UK, USA: Momentum Pictures (UK); Samuel Goldwyn Films (US), 2006.

Arthur, D. (1995). Measurement of the professional self-concept of nurses: developing a measurement instrument. *Nurse Education Today, 15*(5), 328–335.

Aspen Institute. (2008). *Where will they lead, 2008? MBA student attitudes about business and society*. Aspen, CO: A Center for Business Education.

Astin, A. W., & Sax, L. J. (1998). How undergraduates are affected by service participation. *Journal of College Student Development, 39*, 251–263.

Augier, M., & March, J. G. (2007). The pursuit of relevance in management education. *California Management Review, 49*(3), 129–146.

Augier, M., & March, J. G. (2011). *The roots, rituals, and rhetorics of change: North American business schools after the second World War*. Palo Alto, CA: Stanford Business Books.

Badaracco Jr, J. L., & Barkan, I. (2001). Ann Hopkins (A). Boston, MA: *Harvard Business School Publishing* 9-391-155.

Badaracco, J. L., & Harmeling, S. (2002). The individual and the corporation: Kathy Levinson and E*Trade (A). *Harvard Business School Publishing* 9-301-057.

Barger, R. N. (2000). *A summary of Lawrence Kohlberg's stages of moral development.* Notre Dame, IN: University of Notre Dame. Retrieved on August, 12, 2006.

Branagh, Kenneth. *"Henry V."* USA, UK: The Samuel Goldwyn Company (USA), Curzon Film Distributors (UK), 1989.

Barratier, Christophe. *"The Chorus."* France, Germany, Switzerland: Pathe Renn Productions, 2004.

Bazerman, M. H., Loewenstein, G., & Moore, D. A. (2002). Why good accountants do bad audits. *Harvard Business Review, 80*(11), 96–103.

Beer, M, & Rogers, G. C. (1995). Human Resources at Hewlett-Packard (A). Boston, MA *Harvard Business School Publishing* 9-495-051.

Beer, M. & Werssowelz, R. (1982). Human resources at Hewlett-Packard. Boston, MA: *Harvard Business School Publishing* 9-482-125.

Beets, S. D. (2011). Critical events in the ethics of US corporation history. *Journal of Business Ethics, 102*(2), 193–219.

Behrman, J. N., & Levin, R. I. (1984). Are business schools doing their job. *Harvard Business Review, 62*(1), 140–147.

Bennis, W. G., & O'Toole, J. (2005). How business schools lost their way. *Harvard Business Review, 83*(5), 96–104.

Benson, P. G. (2004). The evolution of business education in the U.S. *Decision Line, 35*(2), 17–20.

Bixler, G. K., & Bixler, R. W. (1959). The professional status of nursing. *The American Journal of Nursing, 45*(9), 730–735.

Bolman, L. G., & Deal, T. E. (2013). *Reframing organizations.* San Francisco, CA: Jossey-Bass Publishers.

Bolman, L. G., & Deal, T. E. (2006). *The wizard and the warrior: Leading with passion and power* (Vol. 12). San Francisco, CA: John Wiley & Sons.

Borkowski, S. C., & Ugras, Y. J. (1998). Business students and ethics: a meta-analysis. *Journal of Business Ethics, 17*(11), 1117–1127.

Bowles, S., & Gintis, H. (1976). *Schooling in capitalist America: education reform and the contradictions of economic life.* New York, NY: Basic Books.

Bremer, L. P. (2006). *My year in Iraq: the struggle to build a future of hope.* New York, NY: Simon and Schuster.

Brenner, S. N. (1992). The stakeholder theory of the firm. Retrieved October 28, 2016, http://philpapers.org/

Brint, S. (1996). *In an age of experts: the changing role of professionals in politics and public life.* Princeton, NJ: Princeton University Press.

Browning, L. (2003). Ethics lacking in business school curriculum, students say in survey, *New York Times,* May 20, 2003.

Burke, J. P. (2005). The contemporary presidency: Condoleezza Rice as NSC advisor: a case study of the honest broker role. *Presidential Studies Quarterly, 35*(3), 554–575.

Burns, J. M. (2003). *Transforming leadership: a new pursuit of happiness* (Vol. 213). New York, NY: Grove Press.

Candy, P., Crebert, G., & O'Leary, J. (1994). *Developing lifelong learners through undergraduate education: commissioned report.* Canberra: Australian Publishing Service.

Capra, Frank. *"Why We Fight?".* USA: Disney Studios, 1942-1945.

Carpenter, D. D., Harding, T. S., Finelli, C. J., & Passow, H. J. (2004). Does academic dishonesty relate to unethical behavior in professional practice? an exploratory study. *Science and Engineering Ethics, 10*(2), 311–324.

Cataldi, E., Bradburn, E., Fahimi, M., & Zimbler, L. (2004). *National study of postsecondary faculty (NSOPF: 04): background characteristics, work activities, and compensation of instructional faculty and staff.* Washington, DC: National Center for Education Statistics.

Chandor, J.C. *"Margin Call."* USA: Lionsgate Entertainment, 2011.

Chang, L. T. (2009). *Factory girls: from village to city in a changing China.* Random House Digital, Inc. Retreived, October 24, 2016. www.randomhousedigital. com/

Chitty, K. K., & Black, B. P. (2011). *Professional nursing: concepts & challenges.* Maryland Heights, MO: Saunders/Elsevier

Coalition for Civic Engagement and Leadership. (2007). About us Definitions. Retrieved October 24, 2016.terp.umd.edu/

Cohen, Helen A. *The Nurse's Quest for a Professional Identity.* Addison-Wesley, 1981.

Colby, A., Ehrlich, T., Sullivan, W. M., & Dolle, J. R. (2011). *Rethinking undergraduate business education: Liberal learning for the profession* (Vol. 20). San Francisco, CA: Jossey-Bass.

Cole, T. R., Carlin, N. S., & Carson, R. A. (2014). *Medical humanities: an introduction.* New York, NY: Cambridge University Press.

Cone, R. E., Kiesa, A., & Longo, N. V. (2006). *Raise your voice: a student guide to making positive social change.* Providence, RI: Campus Compact.

Cooper, D. R., Schindler, P. S., & Sun, J. (2006). *Business research methods.* New York, NY: McGraw-Hill

Cowin, L. (2001). Measuring nurses self-concept. *Western Journal of Nursing Research, 23*(3), 313–325.

Crainer, S., & Dearlove, D. (1999). *Gravy training: inside the business of business schools.* San Francisco, CA: Jossey-Bass.

Crane, R. S. (1968). *The idea of the humanities and other essays.* Chicago, IL: University of Chicago Press.

Creswell, J. W. (2009). *Research design: qualitative, quantitative, and mixed methods approaches.* Los Angeles, CA: Sage Publications, Inc.

Cronin, T. E. (2009). The liberal arts and leadership learning (pp. 37–53). In Wren, J. T., Riggio, R. and Genovese, M., *Leadership and the Liberal Arts*: New York, NY: Palgrave Macmillan.

Cummings, L. (1990). Reflections on management education and development: drift or thrust into the 21st century? *The Academy of Management Review, 15*(4), 694–696.

Currie, G., Davies, J., & Ferlie, E. (2016). A call for university-based business schools to "Lower Their Walls": collaborating with other academic departments in pursuit of social value. *Academy of Management Learning & Education*, 2015.0279.

Curry, L., & Wergin, J. F. (1993). *Educating professionals. Responding to new expectations for competence and accountability.* San Francisco, CA: Jossey Bass.

Damon, W. (2009). *The path to purpose: how young people find their calling in life.* New York, NY: Free Press.

Davila, A., Foster, G., & Hoyt, D. (2008). San Diego Padres: PETCO Park as a catalyst for urban redevelopment. Stanford, CA: *Stanford Graduate School Case* SPM-37.

Dolev, J. C., Friedlaender, L. K., & Braverman, I. M. (2001). Use of fine art to enhance visual diagnostic skills. *JAMA, 286*(9), 1020–1021.

Donaldson, T., & Preston, L. E. (1995). The stakeholder theory of the corporation: concepts, evidence, and implications. *Academy of management Review, 20*(1), 65–91.

Drucker, P. F. (1968). The graduate business school. *Fortune, 42*(August), 92–94.

Drucker, P. F. (1992). *The age of discontinuity: guidelines to our changing society.* Piscataway, NJ: Transaction Publishers.

Duggan, W. (2007). *Strategic intuition: the creative spark in human achievement.* New York, NY: Columbia University Press.

Ehrensal, K. N. (2001). Training capitalism foot soldiers: the hidden curriculum of undergraduate business education. In E. Margolis (Ed.), *The hidden curriculum in higher education* (pp. 97–113). New York, NY: Routledge.

Epstein, D. (2006, March 24, 2006). Rethinking the MBA curriculum, *Inside Higher Education*. Retrieved October 24, 2016. www.insidehighered.com /news/2006/03/24/bschoolFederico, G. (2005).

Feeding the world: an economic history of agriculture, 1800–2000. Princeton, NJ: Princeton University Press.

Ferguson, Charles. *"No End in Sight."* USA: Magnolia Pictures, 2007.

Ferguson, N. (2011). *Civilization: the West and the rest.* New York, NY: Penguin Press.

Fink, L. D. (2013). *Creating significant learning experiences: an integrated approach to designing college courses.* San Francisco, CA: John Wiley & Sons.

Fiske, S. T., Bersoff, D. N., Borgida, E., Deaux, K., & Heilman, M. E. (1991). Social science research on trial: use of sex stereotyping research in Price Waterhouse v. Hopkins. *American Psychologist, 46*(10), 1049.

Foundation, F. (1959). *Annual report.* New York, NY: Ford Foundation.

Freidson, E. (1984). The changing nature of professional control. *Annual Review of Sociology*, 1–20.

Freidson, E. (1994). *Professionalism reborn: theory, prophecy, and policy.* Chicago, IL: University of Chicago Press.

Freidson, E. (2001). *Professionalism, the third logic: on the practice of knowledge.* Chicago, IL: University of Chicago Press.

French, R., & Grey, C. (1996). *Rethinking management education.* Thousand Oaks, CA: Sage Publications Ltd.

Friedman, M. (1970). The social responsibility of business is to increase its profits. *New York Times*, September 13.

Gardner, H., & Laskin, E. (1995). *Leading minds: An anatomy of leadership.* New York, NY: Basic Books.

Garnier, Katja von. *"Iron Jawed Angels."* USA: HBO Films, 2004.

General Management Aptitude Test. (2011). *What corporate recruiters say?* Retrieved April 29, 2012, 2012, from http://www.mba.com/why-b-school/benefits-and-future-value/what-corporate-recruiters-say.aspx

Gentile, M. C. (2010). *Giving voice to values: how to speak your mind when you know what's right.* New Haven, CT: Yale University Press.

Gilbert, N. (2012). African agriculture: dirt poor. *Nature, 483*, 525–527.

Gioia, D. A. (2002). Business education's role in the crisis of corporate confidence. *The Academy of Management Executive, 16*(3), 142–144.

Gladwell, M. (1996). The science of shopping. *The New Yorker, 4*(11), 66–75.

Goode, W. J. (1957). Community within a community: the professions. *American Sociological Review, 22*(2), 194–200.

Gordon, L. (2002). Social movements, leadership, and democracy: toward more utopian mistakes. *Journal of Women's History, 14*(2), 102–117.

Gordon, R., & Howell, J. (1959). *Higher education for business.* New York, NY: Columbia University Press.

Gregg, S., & Stoner, J. (2008). *Rethinking business management: examining the foundations of business education.* Princeton, NJ: Witherspoon Institute.

Grossman, A., Steenburgh, T. J., Mehler, L. S., & Oppenheimer, M. B. (2010). Planned Parenthood Federation of America in 2008. *Harvard Business School Publishing* 9-309-104.

Hall, R. H. (1968). Professionalism and bureaucratization. *American Sociological Review, 33*(1), 92–104.

Hawawini, G. (2005). The future of business schools. *Journal of Management Development, 24*(9), 770–782.

Haywood-Farmer, J., & Stuart, F. I. (1990). An instrument to measure the degree of professionalism in a professional service. *The Service Industries Journal, 10*(2), 336–347.

Heller, N. A., & Heller, V. L. (2011). Business ethics education: are business schools teaching to the AACSB ethics education task force recommendations? *International Journal of Business and Social Science, 2*(20).

Hensel, D. (2009). *The relationships among health status, healthy lifestyles, and nursing self-concept among professional nurses.* (Ph.D. Doctoral Dissertation), Walden University, ProQuest/UMI. (3342474).

HERI. (2012). *College senior survey.* Retrieved November 6, 2011, from http://www.heri.ucla.edu/cssoverview.php

Hexter, J., & Woetzel, J. (2013). *Operation China: from strategy to execution.* Boston, MA: Harvard Business Press.

Howard, Ron. *"Frost/Nixon."* USA: Universal Pictures, 2008.

Huckman, R. S., Pisano, G. P., & Rennella, M. (2007, rev. 2010). Wyeth Pharmaceuticals: Spurring scientific creativity with metrics. Harvard Business School Publishing 9-607-008.

Huckman, R. S., & Strick, E. (2010). GlaxoSmithKline: reorganizing drug discovery (A). Boston, MA: *Harvard Business School Publishing 9-605-072.*

Hugstad, P. (1983). *The business school in the 1980s: liberalism versus vocationalism.* New York, NY: Praeger Publishers.

Imse, T. P. (1962). *The professionalization of business management.* New York, NY: Vantage Press.

Jacoby, B. and Associates. (2009). *Civic engagement in higher education. Concepts and practices.* San Francisco, CA: *Jossey-Bass.*

Jarecki, Eugene. *"Why We Fight?".* USA: Sony Pictures Classics, 2005.

Jensen, M. C. (1994). Self-interest, altruism, incentives, and agency theory. *Journal of Applied Corporate Finance, 7*(2), 40–45.

Johnson, C. E. (2011). *Organizational ethics: a practical approach.* Thousand Oaks, CA: Sage Publications.

Johnson, C. E. (2013). *Meeting the ethical challenges of leadership: casting light or shadow.* Thousand Oaks, CA: Sage Publications.

Johnson, C. E. (2016). *Organizational ethics: a practical approach.* Thousand Oaks, CA: Sage Publications.

Kanter, R. M. (2000). *Men and women of the corporation.* New York, NY: Basic Books.

Kanter, R. M. (2005). *Leadership for change: enduring skills for change masters.* Boston, MA: *Harvard Business School Publishing* 9-304-062.

Kanter, R. M. (2010). *Supercorp: how vanguard companies create innovation, profits, growth, and social good*. London: Profile Books.

Kaplan, R. S., & Taranto, N. (2010). Paul Bremer at the Coalition Provisional Authority in Iraq. Boston, MA: *Harvard Business School Publishing* 9-411-010.

Kellerman, B. (2004). *Bad leadership: what it is, how it happens, why it matters*. Boston, MA: Harvard Business Press.

Khurana, R. (2007). *From higher aims to hired hands: the social transformation of American business schools and the unfulfilled promise of management as a profession*. Princeton, NJ: Princeton University Press.

Khurana, R., and N. Nohria. *"It's Time to Make Management a True Profession."* Harvard Business Review, no. October Issue (2008).

Kiesa, A., Orlowski, A. P., Levine, P., Both, D., Kirby, E. H., Lopez, M. H., & Marcelo, K. B. (2007). Millennials talk politics: a study of college student political engagement. *Center for Information and Research on Civic Learning and Engagement (CIRCLE)*.1-52.

Koehn, N. F. (2011). Leadership lessons from the Shackleton Expedition. *New York Times*.

Koehn, N. F., Helms, E., & Mead, P. (2003). *Leadership in crisis: Ernest Shackleton and the epic voyage of the endurance*. Boston, MA: Harvard Business School Publishing 9-803-127.

Kohlberg, L. (1973). Stages and aging in moral development—some speculations. *The Gerontologist, 13*(4), 497.

Kohlberg, L. (1975). The cognitive-developmental approach to moral education. *Phi Delta Kappan, 56*(10), 670–677.

Kohlberg, L. (1976). Moral stages and moralization: the cognitive-developmental approach. In T. Lickona (Ed.), *Moral development and behavior: theory, research, and social issues* (pp. 31–53). New York, NY: Holt, Rinehart and Winston.

Kohlberg, L., & Candee, D. (1984). The relationship of moral judgment to moral action. In W. M. Kurtines & J. L. Gewirtz (Eds.), *Morality, moral behavior, and moral development*. New York, NY: Wiley.

Kopple, Barbara. *"Harlan County, USA."* USA: First Run Features, 1976.

Krause, E. A. (1999). *Death of the guilds: professions, states, and the advance of capitalism, 1930 to the present*. New Haven, CT: Yale University Press.

Kuhn, T. S. (1970). *The structure of scientific revolutions*. International Encyclopedia of Unified Science. Foundations of the Unity of Science (Vol. 2, no. 2) Chicago, IL: The University of Chicago Press.

Laird, T. F. N., Engberg, M. E., & Hurtado, S. (2005). Modeling accentuation effects: enrolling in a diversity course and the importance of social action engagement. *The Journal of Higher Education, 76*(4), 448–476.

Lan, G., McMahon, S., King, N., & Rieger, F. (2003). Moral reasoning of business, nursing and liberal arts students. *Journal of Business Economics Research, 1*(2), 21–32.

Landsman, M., & McNeel, S. P. (2003). Moral judgment of law students across three years: influences of gender, political ideology and interest in altruistic law practice. *South Texas Law Review, 45,* 891.

Lee, Grace. *"American Revolutionary: The Evolution of Grace Lee Boggs "*. USA: Cherry Sky Pictures; Center for Asian American Media; Chicken & Egg Pictures, 2013.

Legge, J. (2009). *The Confucian analects, the great learning & the doctrine of the mean.* New York, NY: Cosimo, Inc.

Lester, S. (1995). Beyond knowledge and competence towards a framework for professional education. *Capability, 1*(3), 44–52.

Levin, L. A., & Mattis, M. (2006). Corporate and academic responses to gender diversity. *Equal Opportunities International, 25*(1), 60–70.

Liedtka, J. M., & Salzman, R. (2009). *Leading innovation at Kelvingrove (A).* Los Angeles, CA: J. Paul Getty Trust and the University of Virginia Darden School Foundation.

Lipman-Blumen, J. (2000). *Connective leadership: managing in a changing world.* New York, NY: Oxford University Press.

Lipman-Blumen, J. (2006). *The allure of toxic leaders: why we follow destructive bosses and corrupt politicians-and how we can survive them.* New York, NY: Oxford University Press.

Lopez, M. H., Kirby, E., Sagoff, J., & Herbst, C. (2005). *The youth vote 2004 with a historical look at youth voting patterns, 1972–2004.* College Park, MD: Center for Information and Research on Civic Learning and Engagement.

MacDonald, K., & Ritzer, G. (1988). The sociology of the professions. *Work and Occupations, 15*(3), 251–272.

Maciariello, J. A., & Linkletter, K. (2011). *Drucker's lost art of management: Peter Drucker's timeless vision for building effective organizations.* New York, NY: McGraw Hill Professional.

Mackey, J. (2011). What conscious capitalism really is: a response to James O'Toole and David Vogel's "Two and a Half Cheers for Conscious Capitalism." *California Management Review, 53*(3), 83–90.

Mackey, J., & Sisodia, R. (2014). *Conscious capitalism, with a new preface by the authors: liberating the heroic spirit of business.* Boston, MA: Harvard Business Review Press.

March, A., & McCormack, D. (2009). Nursing theory-directed healthcare: modifying Kolcaba's Comfort Theory as an institution-wide approach. *Holistic Nursing Practice, 23*(2), 75–80.

Margolis, E., Soldatenko, M., Acker, S., & Gair, M. (2001). Peekaboo. In E. Margolis (Ed.), *The hidden curriculum in higher education* (pp. 1–20). New York, NY: Routledge.

Marquis, C., Beunza, D., Ferraro, F., & Thomason, B. (2010). Driving sustainability at Bloomberg LP. Boston, MA: *Harvard Business School Publishing* 9-411-025.

Martensson, P., Bild, M., & Nilsson, K. (2008). *Teaching and learning at business schools: transforming business education.* Burlington, VT: Gower Publishing Company.

McCabe, D. L., & Trevino, L. K. (1995). Cheating among business students: a challenge for business leaders and educators. *Journal of Management Education, 19*(2), 205–218.

McCoy, K. *"Madoff Won't Appeal Sentence."* USA Today, no. July 10 (2009): p. 38.

Meade, E., & Weaver, S. (2004). *Toolkit for teaching in a democratic academy.* Allentown, PA: Cedar Crest College.

Menendez, Ramon. *"Stand and Deliver."* USA: Warner Bros., 1988.

Mews, C. J., & Abraham, I. (2007). Usury and just compensation: religious and financial ethics in historical perspective. *Journal of Business Ethics, 72*(1), 1–15.

Miles, M. P., Hazeldine, M. F., & Munilla, L. S. (2004). The 2003 AACSB accreditation standards and implications for business faculty: a short note. *The Journal of Education for Business, 80*(1), 29–34.

Miller, B. (1985). Just what is a professional? *Nursing Success Today, 2*(4), 21.

Millerson, G. (1964). *The qualifying associations: a study in professionalization.* London: Routledge & Kegan Paul.

Mintzberg, H. (2004). *Managers not MBAS.* New York, NY: Berrett-Koehler.

Moore, W. E., & Rosenblum, G. W. (1970). *The professions: roles and rules.* New York, NY: Russell Sage Foundation.

Morrill, R. L. (1982). Educating for democratic values. *Liberal Education, 68*(4), 365–376.

Morris, Errol. *"The Fog of War."* USA: Sony Pictures Classics, 2003.

Muller, Ray. *"The Wonderful Horrible Life of Leni Riefenstahl."* Germany: Arte, Omega Film GmbH ZDF, Kino, 1993.

Musil, C. T. (2005). The civic work of diversity. *Diversity Digest, 9*(1), 1–11.

Musil, C. M. (2006). *Assessing global learning: matching good intentions with good practice.* Washington, DC: Association of American Colleges and Universities.

Narvaez, D., & Bock, T. (2009). *Nurturing character in the classroom.* EthEx Series, Book 2: Ethical Judgment. Notre Dame, IN: ACE Press.

Narvaez, D., & Endicott, L. G. (2009). *Nurturing character in the classroom.* Ethex Series, Book 1: Ethical Sensitivity. Notre Dame, IN: ACE Press.

Narvaez, D., & Lies, J. (2009). *Nurturing character in the classroom.* EthEx Series, Book 3: Ethical Action. Notre Dame, IN: ACE Press

Narvaez, L. (2009). *Nurturing character in the classroom.* EthEx Series, Book 3: Ethical Motivation: Notre Dame, IN: ACE Press.

National Center for Educational Statistics. (2010). *Fast facts.* Retrieved March 19, 2012, from http://nces.ed.gov/fastfacts/

National Leadership Council. (2007). *College learning for the new global century: a report from the national leadership council for liberal education & America's promise.* Washington, DC: Association of American Colleges and Universities.

Niles, J. D. (1983). *Beowulf: the poem and its tradition.* Cambridge, MA: Harvard University Press.

Nino, L. (2011). Ideological and historical challenges in business education. *American Journal of Business Education, 4*(1), 19–28.

Nino, L. S. (2012). *Precursors of professionalism in senior-level undergraduate business students and the implications of these precursors for business education and the profession.* (Ph.D. Doctoral Dissertation), University of California, Riverside, ProQuest/UMI. (3518716).

Nino, L. S. (2013). Precursors of professionalism in college seniors: influence of major, gender, and institution. *Research in Higher Education Journal, 21.*

Nino, L. S. (2014). Precursors of professionalism of business graduates: implications for business education and the profession. *Journal of Academic and Business Ethics, 9.*

Noland, T. G., & Sinclair, D. (2008). AACSB accreditation: symbol of excellence or march toward mediocrity? *Journal of College Teaching & Learning, 5*(5), 25–30.

Nyström, S. (2009). The dynamics of professional identity formation: graduates' transitions from higher education to working life. *Vocations and Learning, 2*(1), 1–18.

Palepu, K. & Kind, L. (2011). VIZIO, Inc. Boston, MA: *Harvard Business School Publishing* 9-110-024.

Pamuk, S. (2010). "Political Economy and Institutions in the Near East Since the Rise of Islam." *Paper given at Conference on Islam and Economic Development: Past and Present, Duke University.*

Parks, S. D. (2005). *Leadership can be taught: a bold approach for a complex world* (Vol. Chapter 9). Boston, MA: Harvard Business Review Press.

Pascale, R. T., & Christiansen, E. T. (2011). *Honda (A) & Honda (B).* Boston, MA: Harvard Business School Publishing 9-384-049 & 050

Pascarella, E., & Terenzini, P. (1991). *How college affects students: findings and insights from twenty years of research.* San Francisco, CA: Jossey-Bass.

Pascarella, E. T., Smart, J. C., Ethington, C. A., & Nettles, M. T. (1987). The influence of college on self-concept: a consideration of race and gender differences. *American Educational Research Journal, 24*(1), 49–77.

Patterson, J. T. (1996). *Grand expectations: the United States, 1945–1974.* New York, NY: Oxford University Press.

Pearson, C. S. (2012). *The transforming leader: new approaches to leadership for the twenty-first century.* San Francisco, CA: Berrett-Koehler Publishers.

Petriglieri, G., & Petriglieri, J. (June 1, 2009). Business schools need a broader mandate. *Business Week.*

Pfeffer, J., & Fong, C. T. (2002). The end of business schools? Less success than meets the eye. *Academy of Management Learning & Education, 1*(1), 78–95.

Pierson, F. (1959). *The education of American businessmen: a study of university-college programs in business administration.* New York, NY: McGraw-Hill.

Piper, T., Gentile, M., & Parks, S. (1993). *Can ethics be taught?: perspectives, challenges, and approaches at Harvard Business School.* Cambridge, MA: Harvard Business Press.

Porter, L. W., & McKibbon, L. E. (1988). *Management education and development: drift or thrust into the 21st century.* Hightstown, NJ: McGraw-Hill.

Quinn, R. E. (2004). *Building the bridge as you walk on it.* San Francisco, CA: Jossey-Bass.

Rawls, J. (1999). *A theory of justice.* Cambridge, MA: Harvard University Press.

Riefenstahl, Leni. *"Triumph of the Will."* Germany: Reichsparteitag-film, 1935.

Reitenauer, V. L., Cress, C. M., & Bennett, J. (2005). Creating cultural connections: navigating difference, investigating power, unpacking privilege. In: C. M. Cress, P. J. Collier, & V. L. Reitenauer. (Eds.), *Learning through serving: a student guidebook for service-learning across the disciplines* (pp. 67–79). Sterling, VA: Stylus, 2005.

Rest, J. R. (1984). The major components of morality. In W. M. Kurtines & J. L. Gewirtz (Eds.), *Morality, moral behavior, and moral development*(pp. 24–38). New York, NY: Wiley.

Rest, J. R., & Narvaez, D. (1994). *Moral development in the professions: psychology and applied ethics.* Hillsdale, NJ: Erlbaum.

Rest, J. R., Narvaez, D., Bebeau, M. J., & Thoma, S. J. (1999). *Postconventional moral thinking: a neo-Kohlbergian approach.* Hillsdale, New Jersey: Erlbaum.

Rest, J. R., Narvaez, D., Bebeau, M. J., & Thoma, S. J.(2000). A neo-Kohlbergian approach to morality research. *Journal of moral education, 29*(4), 381–395.

Roberts, M. J. (1993). The Johnsonville Sausage Co. (A). Boton, MA: *Harvard Business School Publishing 9-387-103.*

Robin, Marie-Mounique. *"The World According to Monsanto."* Framce. Camada. Germany: Arte, NHK BSI, Yleisradio (YLE), 2008.

Schein, E. H., & Kommers, D. W. (1972). *Professional education: some new directions.* London: McGraw-Hill.

Schön, Donald. (1987). *Educating the Reflective Practitioner* San Francisco: Jossey Bass.

Schön, Donald A. (1983). *The Reflective Practitioner: How Professionals Think in Action.* Vol. 5126: Basic books.

Senge, P. M. (2006). *The fifth discipline: the art and practice of the learning organization*. New York, NY: Broadway Business.

Senge, P. M., Smith, B., Kruschwitz, N., Laur, J., & Schley, S. (2008). *The necessary revolution: how individuals and organizations are working together to create a sustainable world*. New York, NY: Crown Business.

Slaughter, S., & Leslie, L. (1997). *Academic capitalism: politics, policies, and the entrepreneurial university*. Baltimore, MD: The Johns Hopkins University Press.

Slaughter, S., & Rhoades, G. (2004). *Academic capitalism and the new economy: markets, state, and higher education*. Baltimore, MD: Johns Hopkins University Press.

Smith, Martin. "The Madoff Affair." USA: PBS Frontline, 2009.

Snyder, T. D., Dillow, S. A., & Hoffman, C. M. (2009). *Digest of education statistics, 2008*. Washington, DC: National Center for Education Statistics.

Spielberg, Steven. *"Lincoln."* USA: Walt Disney Studios, Motion Pictures; 20th Century Fox, 2012.

Starkey, K., & Tiratsoo, N. (2007). *The business school and the bottom line*. New York, NY: Cambridge University Press.

Swanson, D. L. (2004). The buck stops here: why universities must reclaim business ethics education. *Journal of Academic Ethics, 2*(1), 43–61.

Swanson, D. L., & Fisher, D. G. (2008). If we don't know where we're going, any road will take us there. In D. L. Swanson & D. G. Fisher (Eds.), *Advancing business ethics education*. Charlotte, NC: Information Age Publishing.

Swanson, D. L., & Fisher, D. G. (2009). Business ethics education: if we don't know where we're going, any road will take us there. *Decision Line, 40*(4), 10–13.

Swanson, D. L., & Frederick, W. C. (2001). Campaign AACSB: are business schools complicit in corporate corruption? *Journal of Individual Employment Rights, 10*(2), 151–165.

Swanson, D. L., & Frederick, W. C. (2003). Are business schools silent partners in corporate crime? *Journal of Corporate Citizenship, 9*, 24–27.

Terenzini, P., & Pascarella, E. (2005). *How college affects students: a third decade of research*: San Francisco, CA: Jossey-Bass.

Thomas, P., & Hewitt, J. (2011). Managerial organization and professional autonomy: a discourse-based conceptualization. *Organization Studies, 32*(10), 1373–1393.

Tierney, W. G. (1989). *Curricular landscapes, democratic vistas: Transformative leadership in higher education*. Santa Barbara, CA: Greenwood Publishing Group.

Toit, D. (1995). A sociological analysis of the extent and influence of professional socialization on the development of a nursing identity among nursing students at two universities in Brisbane, Australia. *Journal of Advanced Nursing, 21*(1), 164–171.

Trank, C. Q., & Rynes, S. L. (2003). Who moved our cheese? Reclaiming professionalism in business education. *Academy of Management Learning & Education, 2*(2), 189–205.

Trapnell, J. E. (2007). AACSB international accreditation. *Journal of Management Development, 26*(1), 67–72.

Tunstall, T. (2012). *Changing lives: Gustavo Dudamel, El Sistema, and the transformative power of music.* New York, NY: WW Norton & Company.

Vogel, Frank E, and Samuel L Hayes. *Islamic Law and Finance: Religion, Risk, and Return.* Vol. 16: Brill, 1998.

Waley, A. (2005). *The analects of Confucius* (Vol. 28). Newyork, NY: Oxford University Press.

Ward, W. A. (1970). Fountains of faith; the words of William Arthur Ward. Anderson. SC: Droke House;

Wear, D., & Bickel, J. (2009). *Educating for professionalism: creating a culture of humanism in medical education.* Iowa, IA: University of Iowa Press.

White, J. B., Levernier, W., & Miles, M. P. (2005). The unintended effects of the AACSB'S 2003 accreditation standards. *The Coastal Business Journal, 4*(1), 43–50.

Wilbur, J. B. (1984). *The integration of ethics into business education: essays on the SUNY college at Geneseo experience.* Geneseo, NY: State University of New York.

World Resources Institute. (2012). *Feeding the world: disappearing land.* Washington D.C: World Resources Institute, Retrevied October 24, 2016. www.wri.org/publication/content/8326.

Wren, J. T., Riggio, R. E., & Genovese, M. A. (2009). *Leadership and the liberal arts: achieving the promise of a liberal education.* New York, NY: Palgrave Macmillan.

Zheng, S., & Kahn, M. E. (2013). Understanding China's urban pollution dynamics. *Journal of Economic Literature, 51*(3), 731–772.

Zingales, L. (2015). Does Finance Benefit Society?. NBER Working Papers 20894, National Bureau of Economic Research.

Zlotkowski, E. A., Longo, N. V., & Williams, J. R. (2006). *Students as colleagues: expanding the circle of service-learning leadership.* Providence, RI: Campus Compact, Brown University.

Zwick, Edward. *"Glory."* USA: TriStar Pictures, 1989.

Index

THE GIVING VOICE TO VALUES ON BUSINESS ETHICS AND CORPORATE SOCIAL RESPONSIBILITY COLLECTION

Mary Gentile, *Editor*

The Giving Voice To Values initiative teamed up with Business Expert Press to produce a collection of books on Business Ethics and Corporate Social Responsibility that will bring a practical, solutions-oriented, skill-building approach to the salient questions of values-driven leadership. Giving Voice To Values (www.GivingVoiceToValues.org)—the curriculum, the pedagogy and the research upon which it is based—was designed to transform the foundational assumptions upon which the teaching of business ethics is based, and importantly, to equip future business leaders to not only know what is right, but how to make it happen.

Other Titles in This Collection

- *Engaging Millennials for Ethical Leadership: What Works For Young Professionals and Their Managers* by Jessica McManus Warnell
- *Sales Ethics: How To Sell Effectively While Doing the Right Thing* by Alberto Aleo and Alice Alessandri
- *Working Ethically in Finance: Clarifying Our Vocation* by Anthony Asher
- *A Strategic and Tactical Approach to Global Business Ethics, Second Edition* by Lawrence A. Beer
- *Shaping the Future of Work: What Future Worker, Business, Government, and Education Leaders Need To Do For All To Prosper* by Thomas A. Kochan
- *War Stories: Fighting, Competing, Imagining, Leading* by Leigh Hafrey
- *Social Media Ethics Made Easy: How to Comply with FTC Guidelines* by Joseph W. Barnes
- *Adapting to Change: The Business of Climate Resilience* by Ann Goodman

Announcing the Business Expert Press Digital Library

Concise e-books business students need for classroom and research

This book can also be purchased in an e-book collection by your library as

- *a one-time purchase,*
- *that is owned forever,*
- *allows for simultaneous readers,*
- *has no restrictions on printing, and*
- *can be downloaded as PDFs from within the library community.*

Our digital library collections are a great solution to beat the rising cost of textbooks. E-books can be loaded into their course management systems or onto students' e-book readers. The **Business Expert Press** digital libraries are very affordable, with no obligation to buy in future years. For more information, please visit **www.businessexpertpress.com/librarians**. To set up a trial in the United States, please email **sales@businessexpertpress.com**

www.ingramcontent.com/pod-product-compliance
Lightning Source LLC
Chambersburg PA
CBHW070530200326
41519CB00013B/3000